Women and Knowledge in Me

Women and Knowledge in Mesoamerica

From East L.A. to Anahuac

Paloma Martinez-Cruz

The University of Arizona Press • Tucson

The University of Arizona Press

www.uapress.arizona.edu

Library of Congress Cataloging-in-Publication Data

Martinez-Cruz, Paloma.
Women and knowledge in Mesoamerica : from east L.A. to Anahuac / Paloma Martinez-Cruz.
p. cm.
Includes bibliographical references and index.
ISBN 978-0-8165-2942-1 (pbk. : alk. paper)
1. Indian women—Intellectual life. 2. Indian women—Rites and ceremonies. 3. Indian women—Social conditions. I. Title.

E59.W8M37 2011
305.48'89707201—dc23

2011027027

Manufactured in the United States of America on acid-free, archival-quality paper containing a minimum of 30% post-consumer waste and processed chlorine free.

16 15 14 13 12 11 6 5 4 3 2 1

Dedicated to my mother,
Rosa Maria Martinez,
Warrior Woman

Contents

Figures

Acknowledgments

ALTHOUGH MY DEBT OF GRATITUDE to family, friends, and colleagues can never be repaid, a few names must figure here, the entry lions that create and defend a space for me to think and feel. The work that ensues is the sound of their inexhaustible roar: Rosa Ando Martinez, Richard V. Cruz, Camilo Cruz, Emiliano Vargas, Jaime Vargas, Daniel Gallegos, Dominica Rice, Shanna Lorenz, Amado Carrasco, Agustina Martinez, Ana Montalvo, Patricia Osuna, Carlos Cruz, Sophie Hand, Aaron Michael Morales, Carlos Murillo, Paul Martinez Pompa, Corry Banton, Derek Bell, Brant Veilleux, Patricia Carlos, Leonard Dominguez, Irasema Gonzalez, Silvia Rivera, Janet Garcia, Nuco Villanueva, Roxanna Sooudi, Matt Statler, Matt Krystal, Norval Bard, Stephen Macek, Susan Martin Goodrich, beloved *mociuaquetzque,* and Kenneth Cruz, beloved *huitzilli*. Additionally, the generous time and expertise provided by Bruno Bosteels, Diana Taylor, and Jean Franco were crucial to the development of the present work.

My enduring gratitude goes to various organizations and institutions for their support: North Central College, the Department of Chicano Studies at the University of California at Santa Barbara, the Latina/Latino Studies Program at the University of Illinois at Urbana–Champaign, Proyecto Latina, Zen Life and Meditation Center of Chicago, Village Zendo, Zen Center of Los Angeles, the Graduate School of Arts and Sciences at Columbia University, and the Tinker Foundation.

Finally, my gratitude to the Chicago Jesuit Academy, the Daniel Murphy Foundation, and the Thacher School for the spiritual and intellectual sustenance they have provided my family is inestimable and enduring.

Women and Knowledge in Mesoamerica

I

From East L.A.

I am the one who speaks with God and with Benito Juárez.
I am wise even from within the womb of my mother.
I am the woman of the winds, of the water, of the paths,
because I am known in heaven,
because I am doctor woman.
—*María Sabina*

A "Xicanita" Approach

THIS BOOK IS ABOUT the intellectual traditions of Mesoamerican women. When I first wrote this heading, I mistakenly typed "A Xicanita" instead of "A Xicanista Approach," referring to what Ana Castillo calls a "Xicanista," or decolonial mestiza, way of interpreting society and culture to identify and transcend the consequences of colonization in our lives.[1] I smiled to see the diminutive looking back at me from the screen: Xicanita. Of course, my "Xicanita" was a mistake, a false start. This was not the beginning with which I had intended to launch my study of radical feminist epistemology. If anything, academic inquiry, known for its anti-aesthetic language encasing an "objective" approach, has trained us to locate our studies within the anaerobic environment of a criminal trial, and to distance ourselves from any warmth we may have for the subject of our research. As I have received this sort of training, my first impulse was to simply erase the unintended diminutive, but that's when I discovered that it was too dear, and too unruly, to simply excise. In much less time than it took to wonder whether or not an "ita" belonged there, it had attached itself to the page as an emblem of the way truth claims are socially situated. The granting of epistemic authority consolidates power, and a Western education teaches us that power does not look like me, read like me, or refer to itself the way I refer to people like me, with notes of affection, familiarity, and playfulness.[2] The "ita" both challenged and inspired me to wonder at how I have so thoroughly internalized the idea that a serious discussion of epistemic authority is no place for a Chicanita, and it made me ask the following questions: If a Chicanita can't be a thinker in this book, then where?[3] If a Chicanita can't be a thinker, then who?

This book examines the Chicana, Native American, mestiza, and *indígena* consolidation of intellectual authority. If not us, then who is in charge of knowledge? Theories of knowledge are not impartial. In the social context in which I write, as a college professor and cultural critic, the centripetal flow characterizes officially sanctioned epistemic projects. I am calling "centripetal" truth claims those that make the self larger, aggrandize the name, individuate the thinking being. The other kind, the "centrifugal" transmissions of knowledge, privilege performances and practices rather than the person generating a discourse, ceding egocentric recognition in favor of the empowerment of the community. Many have developed reasonable descriptions of what I am calling here centripetal and centrifugal flows of intellectual work, and often the binary oppositions of public and private, masculine and feminine, and archive and repertoire are perfectly adequate. However, I view Mesoamerican women thinkers as people who empower their community members through the performance of healing, which is not necessarily private, employing techniques that are not always gender-specific, and frequently these are not ritualized or repeated to the degree that I would risk discussing theirs as a repertoire of performances. Also, for what I am considering to be a centrifugal flow, there need not be hara-kiri feats of self-effacement. Simply put, it is difficult to find ways to describe intellectual authority in Western terms that do not associate knowledge with political hierarchies. A Chicanita approach? Well, why not? Why can't my framework come from a clowning place, a diminutive place, a mistake-making place?

What we have come to know as "legitimate" epistemic authority in the West is an environment of public, dueling discourses. The feminist philosopher Michèle Le Dœuff observes that an iconic image of

Decartes appears to be amused by the idea that his readers will attempt an interpretation of his work:

> Everyone knows the familiar portrait of Descartes which appears in almost all editions. According to Alain, the philosopher is looking humorously at anyone who is about to give an interpretation of his work and saying: "Another one who is going to get it wrong!" This anecdote contains the whole melancholic odyssey of the history of philosophy as an academic tradition: Descartes is looking at his commentator, not the other way around, and, if the commentator is clear-sighted, he or she will bow and say, "I am not worthy to have a conversation with you, sir" (it is I who am continuing Alain's tale here).[4]

Le Dœuff's imagery dismay with the "melancholic odyssey" of philosophical work was something I had already internalized: that "legitimate" philosophical competency is a frenzied fight club, a shaken fist, a swollen *au contraire, mon frêre*. (And heaven help you if you are a *soeur*). As a Chicana in the university system, in order to perceive a feminine locus of theoretical work, I had to contend with the sedimentation of "I am not worthy to have a conversation with you, sir."

The problem of locating Mesoamerican women thinkers has long been at the forefront of my field of inquiry. As the idea that women of native cultures were devoid of any original and lasting contribution beyond our culinary talents—and tortilla-as-magnum-opus sung to the tune of "Allá en el rancho grande" was not going to cut it—I was a heavily burdened Chicanita. I was born and raised in East Los Angeles, completing high school in a pregentrified Eagle Rock and moving around Highland Park and Lincoln Heights throughout my childhood, depending on where our divorced mother and father resided. Narrow, tar-veined roads with hairpin bends, chicken coops and citrus trees, Spanish bungalows and the wide, concrete channel of the L.A. River formed the backdrop of my childhood.

My father, Richard V. Cruz (1943–93), had majored in philosophy at California State University of Los Angeles before going on to study law and practice that profession, becoming a Chicano rights attorney of some renown. Mario García has published an edited volume of my father's papers, entitled *Chicano Liberation Theology: Writings and*

Documents of Richard Cruz and Católicos por la Raza (2009), which details some of his early Chicano movement activities, such as his role in inciting the Saint Basil's riot that interrupted a televised Christmas Eve mass. My brother Camilo and I never knew when we might be hit with a volley of our father's unsettling questions: Do you believe in time? What is reality? How do you know you're real? He was an atheist in a Catholic, Chicano culture, and although at that time I had been content to defer to the impassioned doctrine delivered by his Catholic mother, he insisted that we engage in debates on the nature of things. Also, his answers to my own questions often proved to be as provocative as the questions he posed. I once asked him if he had a hero, and he answered without hesitation, "Mao Zedong." When I asked him who if not God, then, created the universe, his rapid-fire response was, "Chicanos."

When Dad managed to wrangle a moderately stimulating conversation out of one of my friends (by tenth grade I was usually in the company of Anglo guys who attended community college and read Rimbaud in French, preached about B. F. Skinner, and skipped class to visit museums), he gleefully pronounced him a philosopher. (And I do mean *him*—it was always a male person who won this exalted appellation). From those Northeast L.A. kegger-and-garage-band days, I knew I just had to figure out how to be one of those myself: someone who read lots of important books, had deep thoughts, and seemed to always know when to bust out the most important theories to demolish their opponent in an argument. To round out my education in self-hatred, I was an urban, eastside child during the 1980s, a decade in which Latinos were far from fashionable, and the Valley Girl who frequented the Sherman Oaks Galleria, dressed like a *Breakfast Club* era Molly Ringwald and spoke like Moon Unit Zappa was the reigning queen of youthful Angelino womanhood.

Although I had no access to what I would then have described as Mesoamerican philosophers, our Chicano movement parents provided us with a stream of information about alternative ways to imagine epistemic authority. I was a child when I first came into contact with the concept of the shaman's journey. My mother had long been a participant and occasional staff person in the psychotherapy sessions of Salvador Roquet. Dr. Salvador Roquet coauthored with Dr. Pierre Favreau *Los alucinogenos: De la concepción indígena a una nueva psicoterapia,* in which he described the collaborative investigation of the clinical potential of *psilocibina* (hallucinogenic mushrooms). I was about eight years old when our mother returned from a trip she had taken with Roquet to Huautla de Jiménez in Mexico. She wore a white cotton T-shirt on which was embroidered a cluster of little mushrooms—a free-thinking Puerto Rican mom during the height of Nancy Reagan's War on Drugs campaign. Once ingested, the mushrooms took their host beyond ordinary perception, and Mom claimed that the experience was worth years upon years of conventional therapy (to which she was no stranger). Her journey to Huautla de Jiménez and her work with Roquet had changed her life.

In 1965, Roquet was the head of the mental health department of the Instituto de Seguridad y Servicios Sociales de los Trabajadores and was frustrated that all known methods in psychotherapy met with the same obstacles. With each technique, patients would become blocked by mental and spiritual levels of resistance in their progress. The Argentine Tallaferro School and the psychedelic movement of the United States provided him with a Western theoretical framework that he synthesized with Mesoamerican pharmacology that had been a part of care delivery in the region for thousands of years. He and his staff made their way to Huautla in 1967, where a Mazatec shaman by the name of María Sabina conducted their first mushroom ceremony and became the individual that most informed and inspired Roquet's ensuing research and practice.

When I was just sixteen I participated in a workshop called a *convivencia* (convivial). Roquet had designed a series of exercises that would simulate the effects of the mushroom ceremony. Without the benefit of hallucinogens, he provided participants with an approximation of the stages of the shaman's ecstatic journey, combining indigenous concepts with Western clinical methodology. I recall undergoing strenuous physical activities that at the time seemed completely arbitrary. In a group of about thirteen men and women from Mexico and the United States, we were paired to face each other while kneeling upright on our knees. We were required to whack the ground in front of us repeatedly with a sopping wet towel. I tired very quickly from the exertion of this activity, and staff people took turns visiting me to insist that I try harder to remain upright and to continue whacking. Another group member was overwhelmed with fury and was soon screaming at the top of his lungs as he vented his pain on the towel and the unyielding cement beneath it. Long after everyone else had made peace with their towel, he raged with his entire body and voice until there was nothing left to expel. He lay on the cement sobbing, and staff members helped him up to take him for a personal interview with Roquet. The participant came back to the group later in the day to resume the chores we had to complete: acting out dramatic scenes from our past, wrestling with each other in groups of two, painting our animal nature on long lengths of butcher paper—we never knew what we would be asked to do next. Roquet was an affectionate yet stern presence who appeared and disappeared without warning as we performed our tasks. When he looked at me I felt excited and afraid; eager to do my best yet anxious that under his knowing gaze, my mental health would earn me a poor grade.

At one point, on the second and last night of the weekend-long convivial, we were awakened by the relentless sounds of stereo chaos. Punk rock and speed metal blended unceremoniously with television commercials, militant Nazi marches, symphonies, African drumming—a raging cacophony accompanied us as the staffers led us blindfolded into another room, positioning us in groups of two, propping us against each other back to front on the carpeted floor. We were instructed to inhale and exhale deeply and rhythmically while our partner massaged our sternum with what I considered to be an uncomfortable amount of pressure. I let out a scream that came from the helplessness caused by the weight on my sternum and by being forced to assimilate an invisible stranger's pace of breath. The complete loss of control, the chaos, and the physical imposition of another person controlling the rhythm of my breath worked to break down all my tolerance and led me into despair. I was raw and emotional as the stereo chaos gave way to the softer, more benign sounds of gentle music and the breaking dawn.

Once our blindfolds were removed, we joined Roquet, who was seated on a low sofa at the edge of a blanket. We gathered around the blanket's perimeter after we had finished our drawing and writing assignments. We used crayon on paper to draw pictures of subjects as abstract as "My God," "My Faith," "My Work," and as concrete as "My Mother" or "My Children." I remember feeling an overachiever's sense of pride at having made recognizable likenesses of family members and other images. They did not tend to be as "neurotic" as those of some of my peers, which I managed by shrewdly avoiding the black and red crayons and the use of a palmar grip. But when it was my turn in the hot seat (we took turns in groups of two sitting in the middle with our drawings and family photos spread out around us), Roquet pointed out that I was merely hiding. I was covering up the truth. I was unwilling to look underneath the tip of the iceberg and subject to scrutiny my true emotional world. He did not allow me to leave the hot seat until a new and more precise, yet less perfect, portrait had emerged.

In the native tradition, Roquet held that mental, physical, and emotional healing could never be separate from spiritual healing. He and his colleagues founded a clinic based on indigenous pharmacology and spirituality called the Pyschosynthesis Institute. In *Los alucinógenos,* Dr. Roquet describes the phases of the ecstatic journey upon which the convivial is based. "Chaos," in the sessions in which psychoactive substances are used, is an early stage. In the convivial version—the only one that would be legally permitted within the United States—the chaos state is one of the final phases of the work, and each of the physical and emotional tasks that participants undergo over the course of the weekend is used to break down repressive impulses of the individual's personality in order to be vulnerable to the chaos moment. The exalted state of sensitivity and emotion produced by the different exercises leads to the culmination of the work, a state in which participants experience love as an essential condition of life. For Roquet, "God," "energy," and "love" were equivalent concepts. Healing occurred when participants recognized their ability to invent their lives and become vehicles of transformation.

After Roquet's passing, I volunteered with his daughter Ivon Roquet as a Spanish and English translator and staff person when she visited the United States to hold weekend or day-long workshops. It felt right to be doing what I could to help the Psychosynthesis Institute's representatives that developed mental health programs for incarcerated and migrant farm labor populations as well as attending to the needs of their traditional clients. The sessions were always bilingual, and while the exercises were based on Mesoamerican cosmogony, never was there a politics of trying to exclude or reverse the imprint of Western culture.

Though the work itself met with great success among patients, other entities were highly critical of these advances. In the pages of *Los alucinógenos* Roquet describes his detractors, who resorted to yellow journalism and slurs to discredit his method of therapy. Without giving details, he mentions the sensationalistic press that accused him of leaving clients deranged and psychotic. He also includes photos of his clinic, the Robert S. Hartman Institute, after it had been "closed by the authorities." Between pages 131 and 132, four photographs show rooms that are either padlocked or in disarray, giving us to understand that the "authorities" had ransacked the place and left it to rot.

Roquet's work was a child of the preconquest Americas and, like its colonial antecedents, suffered at the hands of official forms of knowledge that demonize indigeneity. The censorship of the Psychosynthesis School and the illegal status of native ceremonies employing indigenous pharmacology demonstrate that colonial oppression is not a remote memory, but rather a constant threat to the hemispheric knowledge base that promotes spiritual, physical, and mental health despite institutional attempts to hasten its eradication.

To an adolescent exposure to Roquet's methods, add doses of our father's veneration of Carlos Castaneda's "Toltec wisdom path," which he transmitted to us as a generalized animism, a pseudo-worship of wild sage, lizards, box elder, potato bugs, ocean waves, and marijuana. While an awareness of Mesoamerican practices did not erode my notion of the importance of Western philosophical achievements, a recourse to alternative types of consciousness and transcendence managed to form part of my lexicon, and this was attributable to my having been a child of Chicano movement parents.

I left L.A. for college in the early 1990s, when the enactment of affirmative action policies led to the increased representation of Latinos and Latinas in state colleges and universities. The environment in my residence hall my first year at UC Berkeley was one in which many Anglo students felt comfortable pontificating on their view that most of the Latinos did not truly deserve to be there. We were charity cases who had not earned our place in *their* class, but rather stole it from those who were more deserving. By the time I concluded my studies, California voters had passed Proposition 187, which restricted access of undocumented immigrants to schools and hospitals, and then continued on to pass Proposition 209, which ended affirmative action in the state's educational institutions. I had no hemispheric or historical view of intellectual accomplishment with which to shield myself from these debilitating messages about my unwelcome presence as a Latina in California, and about my intellectual aptitude. I realized that I was missing an important aspect of myself, a facet that I truly longed to own. This search was what Ana Castillo describes in *Massacre of the Dreamers* as a question of each one becoming a re-conquistadora, exploring herself as subject through scholarship.[5]

In college I was hungry to reconquer territory that had been systematically devalued or destroyed. I needed to learn from the voices of Mesoamerican and Native American women who spoke for themselves. This led me to concentrate on Latin American literature and Chicano/a studies, where I could learn about ancient and contemporary Mesoamerican thought production, the contributions of Chicana artists and activists in the United States, and feminist theory.

With the frameworks provided by Latin American area studies, Chicano/a studies, global studies, performance studies, and feminist and literary theories, I arrived at the present volume, which submits that indigenous and mestiza women healers are custodians of a hemispheric knowledge base. While some studies investigate the interpretive power of women throughout the course of Mesoamerica's development from colonial times to the present, these will tend to deal almost exclusively with the textual world, which has been accessible only to the most elite segment of Latin American and US Latino society. This is also the problem with compendiums on feminist writing from all over Latin America, which usually exclude the repertoire and performed knowledge, as well as the specificity of Mesoamerican themes. In this regard, my goals and methods collaborate with those found in performance scholarship and anthropology. Ideas on performance theory and cultural anthropology proposed by Richard Schechner, Diana Taylor, and Inga Clendinnen help form my analysis of the intellectual work of Mesoamerican women. In my Mexica, Mazatec, and medical anthropology chapters, fieldwork and ethnography are crucial to recognizing Indian and mestiza women as models of intellectual agency. Arriving at my thesis by way of broad interdisciplinarity, I explore here the notion of medicine as a hemispheric locus of women's ways of knowing.

I am not the first person to notice that the exclusion of Mesoamerican women thinkers from Western academic projects is a consequence of hemispheric colonization. By historicizing representations of women and knowledge, I hope to both decry the paucity of intellectual historiography on women of color and to further the work my elders have dedicated toward the liberation of the Chicana Nation.

Mesoamericanizing Epistemic Authority

"Mesoamerica" became a part of the Latin American lexicon in recent times, when Paul Kirchoff, the renowned Mexican anthropologist, coined the term to discuss the territories in Mexico and Central America in which the ancient Olmec, Toltec, Mayan, Mexica, and other precolumbian cultures developed. I run into the most glaring difficulties with this designation in the chapter dealing with Iberian American knowledge production derived largely from European forms. However, the term as I am using it here is both a political and a cultural one. Concurring with Guillermo Bonfil Batalla's thesis in *Mexico Profundo,* I maintain that Mesoamerica and the West constitute two distinct civilizing projects in the geographical realms of Anahuac, the term I am using to represent the ancient and contemporary regions where the Mesoamerican civilizing project has contributed significantly to a group's cultural cohesion. Envisioning Mesoamerica as a politics of resistance to colonial hegemony rather than as a strict geography, I employ both *Mesoamerica* and *Anahuac* throughout my study to discuss Chicana, Xicana, Central American, mestiza, and indigenous peoples as well as those born of Iberian ancestors who strive to activate Indian and borderlands consciousness in the Americas.

My original plan had been to historicize the philosophical activity of Mesoamerican women. *Philosophy* comes from the ancient Greek *philos* (loving) and *sophos* (wise one, sage). Pythagoras was the first person to describe himself as a philosopher, presumably because it would have been immodest to claim that he was, himself, wise. Although his term has been a source of contention since its inception, I will hazard an observation about a few of the characteristics that have traditionally distinguished philosophers from the rest of the intellectual specializations. First, philosophers have to be unsatisfied with myth and tradition. Next, philosophers must author a discourse. Finally, philosophers need to test their discourse publicly.

I am not the first person to wonder whether or not indigenous Mesoamerica can be said to have developed philosophical thought according to these criteria. For one example, we can look to Miguel León-Portilla's investigation of precolumbian Mexica thought (also called "Aztec" or "Nahuatl") in which he answers this question affirmatively, based on this group's dissatisfaction with theistic explanations of truth and nature. "If the Nahuatl wise men had done nothing more than create and preserve a rich mythology, their thought could not be discussed as philosophy. For although myths and beliefs constitute the primary attempts to solve the mysteries of the universe, true philosophic development requires conscious and formal inquiry."[6] For León-Portilla, "true philosophic development" breaks away from theism; he aligns his interpretation of philosophy with the Western project that rejects the existence of the divine based on a lack of evidence. If we, like León-Portilla, apply Comtean criteria to determine whether or not Mesoamerican women have ever sent a philosopher down the pike, then we subscribe to remnants of the notion that the evidentialist challenge to theistic thought is the hallmark of humanity's intellectual progress, that primitive societies resort to supernatural explanations, and that empirical-critical cultures are the only ones that have managed to achieve cognitive maturity. By trying to locate Mesoamerican analogues to Western thought production, I had been colluding with the colonizer's ideas of, well, ideas.

The route to epistemic legitimacy, I believed, would be to help the Mesoamerican women's team produce a contender who could last three rounds in the ring with a Thales or a Thoreau. I would borrow from philosophy's glory to clothe the naked indigenous woman, drape her in Greek tunics and have her shine, thus costumed, a triumphant Olympian, as good as the Greeks. Perhaps not a tributary to the evolution of Western truths, but at least a separate but equal development that had been tragically cast aside like Troy's Cassandra, fated to have her theoretical work fall on deaf ears, waiting for posterity to rescue her singular lucidity from obscurity. I was going to build a bridge of similes connecting my dark-skinned Cassandra to the irreducible foundation of all the things that we think and do: as good as, just like, comparable to . . . surely a project elevating Mesoamerican women philosophers to place them alongside the early Western ones was a worthwhile undertaking. I was on my way from East L.A. to Mount Olympus!

But something funny happened on the way to the forum. The women I study here most vigorously represent spiritual authority, and this is a difficult thing for (my) Western mind to value, given the trend of the total dismissal of theistic thought. I find David Abram's work about the demotion of healers, shamans, sages, and Third World mystics helps bring to light the underpinnings of the deeply entrenched shame associated with hemispheric traditions. Abram argues that a medicine person's primary allegiance must be to "the earthly web of relations in which that community is embedded."[7] In other words, a healer's relationship to the natural world is what provides him or her with the skills necessary to cure. The conception that the human group is subordinate to the natural order is precisely what makes this person "worthless" in the Western view.

Abram reasons the subordination of shamanic knowledge by Western hegemony is tantamount to the subordination of nature. "Wellness means a state of balance with the ecological community, while pathology is defined by the lack of balance between self and natural surroundings. However, in a Western assessment of advanced cognition, human pursuits are thought to be superior to a sense of duty and allegiance to the "primitive" animism of Third World healers. Hierarchy, rather than equilibrium, is the ordering that Western institutions consolidate in their granting of epistemic authority. The centrifugal transmission of knowledge performed by Mesoamerican women, according to the philosophical legacy of the colonizer, is devoid of any real intelligence, because it holds that nature is at least as significant as the self.

By Mesoamericanizing my definition of knowledge to allow that it can be derived of the ecological world, I had to move away from the secular humanist projects of Western philosophy that would only serve to undermine my journey toward the restoration of a native knowledge base. I needed to discuss healers, sages, and shamans, and also to explore the religiosity that the native "wise one" designation evokes. Rather than "intellect," "wisdom" has a higher value in cultures that esteem equilibrium over hierarchy. The word *wise* comes into contemporary usage via Old Saxon. Before that, it was a proto-Germanic expression meaning "to see the way." The word is also the ancestor of *vision*—the physical sense that permits us to distinguish between light and dark. Someone with this sense has the knowledge of the right direction, the appropriate course to take. As a suffix, "-wise" continues to construe a given orientation, or the way one may travel. *Clockwise* means the direction in which the hands of the clock turn, and *otherwise* means the other direction—the one that is different or opposite to the one that has been traversed. Both "women of direction" and "women of vision" are connotations that the ensuing chapters corroborate.

I needed a context in which to discuss Mesoamerican women and knowledge, so I chose the long historical view to organize my study. I begin with my chapter entitled "Women Healers of Tenochtitlan." Virtually every Chicana feminist has turned her critical eye toward ancient Mesoamerica to learn from the indigenous civilizations that were conquered and enslaved to pave the way for New Spain's colonial period. Coursework on pre-Hispanic cultures is a requirement for most Chicana and Chicano studies majors and concentrators, indicating the centrality of Mesoamerican studies to the contemporary Chicano identity. For feminists, this will also entail a working understanding of the gender debates regarding preconquest Mexican womanhood.

Midwives in the Postclassic Mexica Empire mastered scientific knowledge and championed women's ways of knowing in the arenas of healing and civic ritual. When a woman did not survive childbirth, the midwives had to defend her corpse from young warriors or sorcerers who hoped to carve away a relic from her lifeless body. During the Ochpaniztli ceremony, midwives were called on to inaugurate the war season by chasing warriors of all ranks through the streets with blood-soaked brooms. These moments of civic spectacle reveal a carefully guarded feminine knowledge base to which midwives claimed exclusive access. However, this knowledge path was obstructed by the glorification of the masculine warrior paradigm that was the most exalted expression of Mexica identity. Within a society that relied on constant military campaigns to preserve and expand its dominance in what is today Mexico's central plateau, during specific moments in the Mexica ritual calendar the warrior male fully submitted to the imposing strength of the female medical specialist in plain and public deference to the mysterious power of women's procreative abilities.

The second chapter, "Plotting Prospero's Daughters," discusses women's access to the production of knowledge in postconquest New

Spain, where even elite women were barred from obtaining university instruction and participating in public discourse. The Counter-Reformation environment permitted a limited space for women's self-expression, which was the spirituality of affective mysticism. While a few prominent nuns managed to emerge from Inquisitorial hearings with their sanctity intact, a great number were punished for pushing the license of mystical raptures too far. Additionally, we have the rare exception of Sor Juana Inés de la Cruz, who championed women's rights to intellectual work only to be betrayed by her confessor and banned from the activity of writing and study. The chapter concludes with a discussion of the Mexican Republic's hindrance of women's suffrage, as women struggled to be recognized as citizens in the nation of their birth. When voting rights were finally conferred, it was not because Mexico had moved toward a democracy, but rather the exact opposite: individual voting power had already been rendered powerless by the increasingly corporatized political culture. As a representative modernity, the category of Mexican national inclusion is discussed as one way in which Mesoamerican peoples experienced enfranchisement, and exclusion, by the postcolonial political structures that were ill prepared to impose a Western grid of meaning on an economically and ethnically heterogeneous region.

In "Survivor Woman," instead of looking at the legacy of peninsular and criolla women, I examine the survival of Mesoamerican medical practices in the New World that have weathered the apocalypse of colonization. In the beginning, factors such as the scarcity of resources, cultural biases, attitudes about race, and the efficacy of Mesoamerican health care encouraged the isolation and continuity of indigenous medicine, but in recent times, the biomedical professionalization or corporatization of Mexico's health sector aggressively erodes Mesoamerican knowledge and care.

Next, "AluciNet.*ion*: Spiritual Capital in the Sierra Mazateca" introduces globalization scholarship and performance theory to interpret the role of Mazatec Mexican women in the advent of spiritual tourism. For this chapter, I have explored Álvaro Estrada's biography of the renowned Mazatec shaman María Sabina for information on the early participation of foreigners in the Mazatec mushroom ritual. Also, thanks to the friendship and hospitality extended to me by Agustina Martínez, a shaman who resides and practices in the Mazatec highlands of Huautla de Jiménez, I have conducted fieldwork that has compelled me to rethink my own essentialist attitudes about indigeneity and authenticity.

"Contesting the Pathogen Myth: Chicano Literature as Curative" examines the representation of wise women from the Chicano movement and beyond. Mainstream US depictions of Latinas treat their presence as it would an infestation: there are too many of them, they are coming too fast, they breed too quickly, and they are by nature parasitic. The figure of the *curandera* is central to Chicano cultural production, because it contests these racist attitudes and celebrates Mesoamerican women as physicians rather than pathogens. I read Rudolfo Anaya's *Bless Me, Ultima* (1971), Ana Castillo's *So Far from God* (1993), and Luis Alberto Urrea's *The Hummingbird's Daughter* (2005) against the background of immigration policies and border images to show how representations of Mexican American women healers restore dignity to a maligned conception of indigenous womanhood.

And so my journey to locate our thinkers, rather than conducting me to the rarefied environment of Apollonian dueling discourses, took me to homes with packed-earth floors, corrugated-aluminum roofs, and mild coffee sweetened with piloncillo, and to city centers with names that were ancient by the time the Mexica arrived to shake their fists at the neighboring kings. Not to Rome or Greece or Walden Pond, but to Anahuac, a borderless inheritance of values and concepts that began with the domestication of maize, and races with its descendants into this new millennium.

The ensuing chapters demonstrate that gender, race, class, and the epistemic privileging of centripetal knowledge production impede our ability to recognize Mesoamerican women as models of intellectual agency. However, restoring submerged, indigenous healing practices is not an exercise in cataloguing "primitive" knowledge systems. Rather, the process of recovering Mesoamerican thinking celebrates living hemispheric curatives that contribute to the alleviation of Western pathologies such as destructive consumerism and planetary greed. The preservation and perpetuation of Mesoamerican medicine must not be regarded as an effort to freeze women into museum dioramas: centrifugal acts of knowledge transmission must be considered in order to imagine a world in which equilibrium, rather than dominance, marks the core value of the enlightened mind.

2

Women Healers of Tenochtitlan

BEFORE COLUMBUS SAILED THE OCEAN BLUE, Inti's yellow rays fell on the fertile contours of Pacha Mama. The sacred *Popol Vuh* taught how humankind was fashioned from maize. Deer Mothers marked spirals and diagonals in the powdery snow, and Buffalo Woman gave meat and fat to her tribe in times of lack. Incas, Mayas, Taos, Comanche: these and many other cultures populated the Americas before the arrival of the Spaniards. The Nahuatl speakers that Hernán Cortés and his allies conquered in 1521 are known as the "Aztecs," but back then, as today, the members of the group that Cortés subdued referred to themselves as "Mexica," so that is what I call them in this chapter. For many people of Mesoamerican descent, to glimpse the imprint of the Mexica Empire on the history of our hemisphere is to detect an ancient aspect of ourselves, a mirror shard that recalls our indigenous past and reminds us that the continent was far from empty when Columbus finally set foot on dry land.

The medicine women among the Mexica led lives in which they publicly pursued scientific innovation, held offices of liturgical and spiritual authority, and championed women's ways of knowing in the arena of civic ritual. However, their prospects as women thinkers were obstructed by the paradigm of masculine warriorhood that dominated the Mexica culture during its Postclassic period. Women healers were not only physicians, but also the national defenders of a feminine knowledge base that warriors attempted to appropriate and manipulate toward their own ends. In precolumbian Mesoamerica, women articulated their own ways of knowing through a repertoire of performances. State and household rituals transmitted gender-specific knowledge systems and protected feminine medical specialization from encroachment by the warrior paradigm.

My information about women healers comes from Spanish chronicles dating from the sixteenth and seventeenth centuries. I would be remiss not to provide the customary note of caution that accompanies any construal of Mexica culture based on the ethnohistories compiled by early Spanish colonizers. These sources are fraught with complications. For example, early European theologians recorded the views of individuals who were asked to submit memories and interpretations of an empire that had just recently fallen under the sword and cross of Spaniards. Hindsight—and most certainly foresight as well—had to have played a role in what they chose to divulge to the Spaniards to whom they were subordinate. Also, textual "memories" invariably reflect the desires of their authors, compilers, and editors. Unlike material culture, such as the archaeological information supplied by burial sites, temple mounds, and sculpture, texts are very selective, and subject to the scrutiny of clerics who were pivotal to the eradication of the old ways. Additionally, the Spanish chroniclers were male, often celibate, and inscribed in a Roman Catholic gender system that presumed the innate corruptness of womanhood. These Spanish newcomers were unqualified to detect, much less sympathize with, the existence of a feminine base of knowledge in the Americas.

Three postconquest chroniclers are central to this research. The Franciscan friar Bernardino de Sahagún compiled invaluable data on the Mexica Empire from Nahuatl speakers reporting on the precontact world. By 1569, all twelve of Sahagún's books were available in Nahuatl. The manuscript is called the *Florentine Codex,* or *The General History of the Things of New Spain*. The Dominican friar Diego Durán conducted interviews with Nahuatl-speaking respondents in the sixteenth century and transcribed these with generous editorial interventions and interpretations. Notably, he believed that American Indians were descended from the lost tribes of Israel, and he drew frequent comparisons between Mexican Indian and Jewish rites that he observed and recorded in his volumes today known as *History of the Indies of New Spain, The Ancient Calendar,* and *Book of the Gods and*

Rites. Nearly one hundred years later, Hernando Ruíz de Alarcón's *Treatise on the Heathen Superstitions That Today Live among the Indians Native to This New Spain* (1629) catalogued Mexica customs, to denounce and eradicate what he considered to be idolatrous and heathen practices. Obviously we are peering at the Mexica universe through the lens of partisan instruments of indigenous assimilation. My interpretation is, of necessity, a speculative reconstruction of Mexica womanhood in which I piece together strewn negative spaces left by millennia of male institutional interests in order to re-member neglected feminine forms.

It is important to emphasize that the Mexica worldview and women's roles within it are not examined here for the exercise of cataloguing a bygone society's attitudes toward gender. We cannot reasonably dismiss the Mexica, and later the Spanish, ways of submerging and silencing Indian women's ways of knowing as being distant in time or space, given that equivalent acts of omission and excision continue to take place today in our own governments, schools, homes, and like arenas. As a project of decolonial scholarship, the retelling of the Mexica conception of gender is a strategy to challenge the Western exclusion of Mesoamerican women's philosophical traditions and restore a silenced intellectual heritage.

In the Days of the Eagle and the Cactus

The available data on the peopling of the Americas reads as a mystery novel that is missing the greater part of its pages. What its devoted readership concludes from the extant chapters tends to be based as much on imperfect scientific evidence as on political partisanship. Western empiricism contends that the first inhabitants arrived anywhere between twelve thousand and one hundred thousand years ago. Native cultures, at odds with Western ciphers, relay an entirely different relationship to the time/space continuum and generally regard with trepidation the din that non-Indians raise about what the presence or absence of bones "proves" about their origins. From the Western perspective, the domestication of corn and other crops meant that Mesoamerican cultures could live in agricultural communities instead of constantly moving in pursuit of game and hospitable environs. By around 6500 BCE, agricultural development focused on maize, beans, squashes, cotton, and chili peppers. The successful yield of crops prompted village formation and cults associated with rain and fertility, complete with ceremonial centers and burial mounds. By 1500 BCE, the rise of the Olmec civilization witnessed the appearance of Mesoamerica's first monumental architecture. To live in urban environments, groups had to develop systems for the demarcation of boundaries and the distribution of resources among different socioeconomic factions, and to make decisions about lines of succession to power and property. Instead of hunter-gatherer or village-organized groups, the Olmecs marked the emergence of state-organized societies.

In 1350 CE, an impoverished Chichimec (Aztec) group settled in the fertile central plateau of what is modern-day Mexico.[1] After its split from the other Chichimec bands, this group, called the Mexica, soon distinguished itself as a force to be reckoned with, and its warriors represented the pinnacle of this culture's pact with the divine. The elevation of the warrior paradigm was one among many aspects of the Mexica society compelling scholars to acknowledge that theirs was stratified according to patriarchal principles. Men expected women to be chaste, modest, submissive, and monogamous, while men could have an array of lovers; female adultery was punished harshly, while a married man could respectably be promiscuous, as long as the women he touched were unmarried (i.e., not someone else's property); women were handed out as spoils among nobles and warriors; they played no visible role in the governing of the state. Indeed, the title "He Who Speaks" (Huey Tlatoani) was conferred on their highest ruler, while women were entirely barred from the world of public address. Although this disdain for women's ways of knowing limited their participation in intellectual projects, my research reveals that women healers exercised a qualified level of epistemic authority.

Women referred to as physicians (*ticitl* in the singular, *titicih* in the plural) practiced in many fields of specialization, from fortune-telling hucksters to acclaimed surgeons. The difference between a capable healer and her fraudulent counterpart is well drawn in the *Florentine Codex*. Under the heading "Physicians," the chapter speaks of the knowledge, experience, and professionalism of a competent doctor.[2] Women doctors are discussed in a tone that conveys respect and gratitude for their services. The narrative associates capable women physicians with knowledge that is acquired through "examinations," "experience," and "professional skill": medical training in which women acquired what was widely perceived to be legitimate competency. And then the text arrives at the description of the bad practitioner: no experimentation, no professionalism, just the sleight-of-hand and fortune-telling tricks that one might expect from a barking carny manning the snake oil booth.

Intriguingly, the codex characterizes the bad woman physician as having "a vulva, a crushed vulva, a friction-loving vulva" and says that she is "a doer of evil." While the good physician is heiress to a tradition of rational inquiry and scientific foundations, the bad physician is the hapless owner of itchy and misshapen genitalia. Presumably, both women would have had vulvas, but only that of the bad ticitl is mentioned specifically. The passage portrays the relationship between knowledge and the "bad" vulva, implying the two are mutually exclusive. In the Mexica Empire, sexual deviance, represented here by the bad ticitl's excessive enthusiasm for friction and her vulva's aberrant shape, was closely linked to cosmic corruption. Alfredo Lopez Austin discusses the conflation of sexuality and sin in Mexica culture, arguing that, as with Christianity, the two are closely related, noting that "the metaphor in teuhtli in tlazolli ('dust, garbage') meant carnal sex in its generic and specific aspects to the ancient Nahua."[3] Women physicians that garnered professional trust and admiration had to behave in strict accordance with the social norms of feminine sexuality, which condemned lesbians, androgynes, and women who demonstrated overt appetites. The *Florentine Codex* makes it clear that to be a woman of knowledge, a physician needed to exhibit unimpeachable temperance: her conduct was as much a part of her professionalism as her cures. By drawing these contrasts, it becomes clear that the mastery of scientific knowledge was an exclusive professional field that welcomed certain women, and it was defined by a code of conduct as well as the successful treatment of patients.

We are told in Hernando Ruiz de Alarcón's *Aztec Sorcerers in Seventeenth Century Mexico: The Treatise on Superstitions* that the word *ticitl* could mean either a man or a woman in Nahuatl, the main language of the Mexica Empire.

> Now getting down in detail to the charms and frauds with which the ones called ticitl deceive and derange . . . we shall first deal with childbirth, by which mankind enters and partakes of the miseries of life. Because of its circumstances, this office is carried out in all nations by women. It is the same with the Indians: the name ticitl includes them, but they are also called tepalehuiani, which means "helper." What in our language means "midwife" is called temexiuitiani in their tongue; while this name is more fitting, they very seldom use it.[4]

What Ruíz de Alarcón lacks in joie de vivre he makes up for by providing a valuable insight about women who practiced in the field of medical specialization that the West today classifies as gynecology and obstetrics. This passage significantly points out that women were the exclusive authorities in the science of birthing.

Mexica midwives plied their trade in a specific political and religious context that favored the contributions of men and elevated the attributes of masculinity. Politically speaking, the Mexica found themselves in a fiercely contested territory in which access to scarce resources, such as arable land and water, was dictated by the supremacy of their warriors. Accordingly, their system of beliefs subordinated women's procreative capacity to men's ability to destroy enemies.

War as the state priority had particular implications in the casting of women's roles. Anthropologist Marvin Harris asserts that wherever conditions favored the intensification of warfare among hunter-gatherer societies, the subordination of women also became more intense. But what about state-organized societies and the professionalization of war, in which an elevated warrior class would have meant that women did not necessarily share a roof and a bed with a man whose civic identity hinged upon his physical dominance, but might just as easily have been a merchant or a farmer or a scribe? In state-organized societies, the subordination of the feminine principle grew out of a particular set of circumstances. Harris points out that women in certain West African cultures were not burdened with many of the customs so frequently observed in patriarchal societies. For example, clubs and secret societies could mobilize to seek redress on behalf of a wronged woman. The Igbo women of Nigeria met in council to discuss their interests as traders, farmers, or wives. If a man violated their market rules or abused his wife, he risked becoming the subject of group retaliation. A group of women would bang on his hut in the middle of the night, sing in a chorus to mock his virility, and turn his backyard into a latrine until he agreed to change his ways. They called it "sitting-on-a-man."[5]

Harris's example of the West African Igbo gives us a view of near gender parity in a state-organized society and demonstrates that maleness is no universal guarantee of impunity. Although the highest rulers in West African kingdoms were nearly always males, the recognition of women's authority and autonomy pervaded domestic and commercial settings.

At first glance, it would seem that the Mexica society met all the requisite conditions for gender parity to thrive. In precolumbian Tenochtitlan, women were not without vital production tasks. Girls were instructed to weave from an early age to contribute to the economy of the household. Women who were highly skilled weavers could externalize their creativity while ensuring financial security. Destined for display as the insignias of warriors, or on the *huipil* dresses to be worn to the marketplace, the products of their weaving, spinning, and embroidery were significant markers of Mexica identity as well as valuable commodities. In the household, women rose early to grind the maize flour that they would turn into tortillas and tamales to nourish the family. Women could be vendors in the marketplace and sell food and clothing. They were valued as mothers and wives and held important offices as healers and priestesses. In all these ways, women complemented the masculine project of nation building as productive and respected counterparts.

Harris proposes that for a state to subscribe to a strongly patriarchal mind-set, it must have survival-sustaining tasks of which men, because of their size and strength, are more capable. As Mesoamerica had no large livestock for milking or slaughter such as cows, sheep, goats, or pigs, and they lacked beasts of burden such as oxen, horses, and mules, there would have been no preference in terms of the muscle mass and size advantage of males to provide base sustenance. Most of their diet of maize, beans, squash, and chilies was farmed on the soft beds of floating gardens called *chinampas*. Without benefit of plows or wheels, the chinampas were soft enough so that it was possible to plant crops with nothing more than digging sticks. In short, the Central Mexican environment did not seem to be one that would favor the physical attributes of maleness for group survival, since both household economy and cultivation of the basic food supply might have been carried out by women.

Applying Harris's model to the setting of metropolitan Tenochtitlan, it stands to reason that if physical strength was not crucial to basic food production, the Mexica must have relied on masculinity to achieve the military expertise that ensured their survival and ascendancy. The mythohistorical narrative of their geographical origin is replete with bellicose metaphor. They began in Aztlán (place of whiteness), an island surrounded by reeds set in the middle of a lake. Obeying the command of their patron deity, Huitzilopochtli (Hummingbird of the South), they followed his priests to the shore of the lake to begin their wanderings on a restless quest for their new home. The welcome they received from the cluster of independent city-states that dotted the Central Valley when they arrived was less than cordial. One Mexica ruler was sacrificed by the Tepanecans; and the mighty Culhuacans, the most prestigious and prosperous group in the region, scornfully invited them to settle in a region called Tizaapan: "Tizaapan was a wilderness, occupied only by vipers and poisonous snakes that came down from the hilltop. This site was given with malice on the part of the advisers of the king. But [the Aztecs] accepted the favor and occupied Tizaapan."[6] The Mexica not only survived in this desolation; they managed to thrive. Astonished by their resourcefulness and strength, the Culhuacans ventured to make a gesture of amity. When the Mexica priests requested that their ruler, Achitometl, give his daughter to be mistress of the Mexica and bride of their god, Achitometl consented, arriving to his daughter's wedding ceremony eager to witness this auspicious union. On the orders of Huitzilopochtli, they sacrificed Achitometl's daughter, and a priest donned her flayed skin for the "wedding" in which his daughter was transformed into Toci (Our Grandmother), a principal goddess who was co-identified with the tenet of discord. Achitometl, quite possibly the most disappointed father of the bride our world has ever known, made war with the Mexica, and they once again found themselves chased off by powerful prior occupants of the plateau. As Huitzilopochtli explained to the high priests, theirs was not to be a society founded on diplomacy and symbiosis, but rather one based on warfare and domination.

After more wandering, they found precarious footing in swampy, hostile terrain in the middle of Lake Texcoco. They knew that the region sat in the middle of where the boundaries of Azcapotzalco and Tezcoco territories coincided, but their resolve to make a permanent home on the lake had been divinely conceived. Once again surrounded by water and reeds that evoked the memory of Aztlán, they saw the sign their priests had foretold: an eagle with its wings outstretched, perched on a prickly pear cactus with a bird in its talons. (In other versions the eagle holds a snake.) Upon seeing the retinue arrive, the eagle bowed its head in their direction.[7]

With this portent they concluded over two hundred years of wandering that had begun in Aztlán and initiated the history of the capital city of the Mexica Empire, Tenochtitlan. The eagle perched on the cactus had been Huitzilopochtli's message to them that they had finally arrived. By that time, conquest and warfare, and thereby the exaltation of masculinity, had already been inscribed as the insignias of the Mexica state.

As for early Mexica cosmogony, they believed the universe was composed of many layered dimensions in which the feminine principle constituted the unpredictable, and therefore dangerous, aspect of the human condition. Human time and space were conceived as the midpoint between temporal meridians, subject to the constant peregrinations of beings that ascended and descended along the thirteen celestial and nine infraterrestrial levels.[8] Each horizontal was populated by gods and lesser supernatural entities. The earth was a flat plane supported by four trees, one in each of the cosmic directions, with a precious green stone at the center. There lived the ancient god, the mother and father of all gods and the principle of duality. Its name was Ometéotl.

The mother aspect of Ometéotl was called Omecihuatl (Lady of Duality), and the paternal was called Ometecuhtli (Lord of Duality). This primordial, multidimensional deity infused the conception of all lower and higher beings. The major gods were known by five different titles that dramatized their distinctive areas of influence. For example, Quilaztli, the goddess of childbirth, was also known as Cohuacihuatl (Woman Serpent), Quauhcihuatl (Woman Eagle), Yaocihuatl (Woman Warrior), and Tzitzimicihuatl (Woman Devil). The quintuple expression of Mexica deity corresponds to the earth's four directions as well as the fifth direction, conceived as a vertical ray connecting the celestial planes and the infernal ones. Standing perpendicular to the earth's surface, each human being marks this cosmic path, as do the anthropomorphic incarnations of the gods.

Between the four trees representing the four cosmic directions and the center, communication was facilitated by *malinalli:* interlaced helixes in constant flux. Humans lived with the anxiety that the malinalli would conduct demonic forces from beyond into the human world. Fountains, forests, mines, and other areas in which the elements of one world seep into the next were considered sites of rupture, reminding humans that only a diaphanous membrane protected their particular dimension, on the other side of which lurked cosmic crisis. Mexica culture was a latticework of rituals and festivals that sought to maintain the stability of their world that, even in its interludes of greatest abundance, was ephemeral and unknowable.

As a group obsessed with the maintenance of balance in a universe in which each polar opposite vied for power, the occult places where the dimensions jutted into each other and eroded the other's integrity were to be feared. As such, woman's reproductive capacity inspired awe, but also dread, since metaphors and rites show us that it represented just such a liminal zone, an unstable conduit, like the malinalli, from which both the blessing of birth and the calamity of death would alternately and unpredictably spring. The following sections detail and interpret the status of women of knowledge, as well as the patriarchal challenges to women's epistemic traditions during the days of the eagle and the cactus.

The Case for Mexica Vulva Envy

In Mexica conception, possession of a vulva (*cihuapilli* or *tepilli*) and womb (*cihuatl* or *tepilixcuatl*) meant that you were a woman. In fact, the word *cihuatl* also meant "woman," fusing the concept of womb and woman in Mexica thought.[9] Mexica titicih had to protect their intellectual tradition that was both derived from, and attending to, woman's reproductive capacity. By investigating cultural attitudes about menstruation in the precolumbian context, we can detect a knowledge base that was particular to the female experience.

As a means to interpret the status of women in a given culture, many anthropologists will examine the way menses is perceived by the group's members.[10] Some mappings of menstrual laws follow Carol Delaney's thesis on Muslim women of Turkey. Delaney identifies the many prohibitions placed on menstruating women, such as touching the Koran, entering the mosque, keeping the fast of Ramadan, or performing the sacred Muslim rituals in the holy precinct of Mecca, as a devaluation of the condition of being female. As the menstruating body is perceived as a danger in the Turkish village, so too are women perceived as having unsafe and unclean bodily boundaries. On the other hand, Thomas Buckley examines traditions among the Yurok women of California and concludes that menstrual laws in this group provide a route to spiritual potency, knowledge, and prosperity.[11] Comparative studies of menses, broadly reviewed, imply that a culture that construes menstrual blood as a pollutant is likely to diminish the status of women, while a culture that understands menstrual blood as pure and sacred will tend to elevate the status of women. The available sources convince me that menstrual blood worked to empower young women in the Mexica setting.

The story of Mexica attitudes toward menses is not an easy one to piece together. Sahagún makes no mention of the menstrual cycle. López Austin, arguably the most accomplished investigator and prolific writer on the Mexica conception of the human body, writes: "Menstruation, in its multiple terms, does not appear etymologically to be thought of as an impurity. The words allude to it simply as a hemorrhage, as a periodic emission, or as an infirmity."[12] In *Aztecs: An Interpretation* (1991), Inga Clendinnen writes, "No special note seems to have been taken of the onset of menstruation . . . that is, no shame appears to have been attached to the simple condition of being female."[13] Apparently, the Mexica women did not undergo stretches of quarantine, ritualistic postmenstrual purifications, or strict prohibitions. If, as many propose, menstruation was not classified as symbolic pollution, then there is room to hypothesize that, as in Buckley's thesis on Yurok beliefs, the Mexica considered this flow to ennoble the condition of being female.

Although my deductions are culled from the dubious material left by Spanish chroniclers, there is one thing we can say with certainty. The paucity of ethnohistories involving menstrual rites simply does not jibe with what we know about blood in the Mexica Empire. If ever a city's works were lubricated by blood, it was that of Classic Tenochtitlan, where the red splash of life was more than just ceremonially significant; it was ubiquitous.

The Spanish called the eighteen major annual ceremonies *veintenas,* as these spanned the length of twenty (*veinte*) days. The veintenas were thought to appease the divine forces that ensured Mexica survival. In the war season, which lasted for nine months of the eighteen-month solar calendar, warriors and priests spilled blood to appease Huitzilopochtli's insatiable thirst on the battlefield. Blood and human hearts fed the sun and earth gods, and it was the unique charge of the Mexica to meet their target hemoglobin quotas at home and abroad. In book 2 of the *Florentine Codex,* examples of the ritual centrality of blood abound. Human hearts were routinely and publicly torn from the chest cavities of slaves, war captives, and prisoners. In the veintena of the second month, called Tlacaxipeualiztli, priests conducted captives to the top of Huitzilopochtli's pyramid, where six priests stretched them across the sacrificial stone and plunged obsidian blades into their chests to extract the hearts.

> And they named the hearts of the captives "precious eagle-cactus fruit." They raised them in dedication to the sun. . . . They offered it to him; they nourished him. . . .
>
> Afterwards they rolled them over; they bounced them down. They came breaking to pieces; they came head over heels; they each came headfirst; they came turning over and over. Thus they reached the terrace at the base of the pyramid.[14]

The oft-repeated municipal spectacle of priests yanking out "eagle-cactus fruit" and offering it to the sun, with the subsequent "bouncing" of the bodies to the foot of the pyramid steps for distribution, served to retell their urgent pact with the gods and enunciate the pivotal role that blood played in normalizing relations with fickle deities.

But blood did not enter into public contemplation only when the priests drew their requisite quantities at the tops of pyramids. Offering blood was also an individual matter, albeit one that, like the pyramidal displays, fell under the definition of civic duty. Every member of the populace—men, women and children alike—were obliged to make regular offerings of blood from their earlobes, tongues, and thighs or shins, from the time of early infancy.

Durán tells us of the veintena held in the fourth month, which was the first occasion in the social life of the Mexica that began to distinguish between male and female blood tribute. Called the "Great Perforation" or "Great Vigil," it served to ritualistically cleanse the mother and child of all the residue of giving birth and being born. All women who had given birth in the previous year were required to place offerings on each shrine leading up to the Great Temple of Huitzilopochtli, where the principal offering took place. Then it was the babies' turn. "On reaching the Temple of Huitzilopochtli, the women took the child, no matter how small, and delivered it to the priest, who took the child and with a stone blade brought by the mother made an incision in his ear and the bud of his virile member. Thus on the ear and on the other place a slight cut was made, so delicate that blood barely came to the surface. The little girls were incised only in the ear."[15] So it was that every last Mexica, no matter how small, was made to produce his or her requisite bleeding for the good of the state. In such a prodigiously sanguine environment, we see that the boys were born owing a blood debt that the girls were not. The boys endured an extra incision that permitted them to emulate the perforation that was already inherent in female anatomy. Here, instead of the Freudian "penis envy" that has long colored Western psychology, we are dealing with a variety of Mesoamerican "vulva envy," with priests carving the imprint of feminine fertility onto the male's body as a first requirement of state membership.

As with the Great Perforation, menstruation presented another occasion for a public display of vulva envy. The same Tocoztli veintena that saw to the perforation of the young also honored Chicomecoatl ("Seven Snake"). Tenochtitlan honored Chicomecoatl (also called Xilonen), the goddess of the harvest, in a pageant of ripening womanhood. Durán describes the wooden representation of the goddess during the season consecrated to her. The figure was ornately carved in the form of a young maiden around twelve years of age. The girl was clothed entirely in red, and her cheeks were rouged. She wore a necklace of golden ears of corn tied with a blue ribbon.[16] The age, colors, and agricultural references to the harvest's yield all collaborate to describe the image of a young woman newly of age. The sustenance conceived by the pairing of human rigors and the caprice of nature is personified here as a young girl issuing the first crimson petals that proclaim her womanhood.

Book 2 of the *Florentine Codex* narrates the procession of young women that carried offerings to the Temple of Chicomecoatl. Feminine fertility is ennobled during this ceremony, when the colors and adornments all call attention to a woman's budding maturity. Red feathers on the girls' arms and legs announced that they were of marriageable age. They carried maize cobs wrapped in paper reddened with liquid rubber, and their cheeks were rouged with iron pyrite.[17]

On the occasions of weddings or during the ritual feast held in honor of Tezcatlipoca, the maidens were called to dance thus adorned to attract the attention of potential suitors. Here, the female actors are described as "young girls," but they are also ready to be married, indicating that they had only recently crossed the threshold into the time of marriageability.

The warrior youths of the city were relegated to a supporting role on this occasion. They accompanied the young women on their trek to Chicomecoatl's temple as escorts but were forbidden to speak with them or distract them from their duty. The codices tell us that the Mexica teens were not so different from the ones we know today—they would not pass up the opportunity to misbehave.

> And if someone joked with one of them, they chid him. One said to him:
>
> "He with the occipital tuft of hair can speak! Canst thou talk? Be thou already concerned over how thy tuft of hair will fall off, thou with the little tuft of hair. It is an evil-smelling tuft of hair, it is a stinking tuft of hair. Art thou not just a woman like me? Nowhere hath thy excrement been burned!"
>
> Some turned on her; they said:
>
> "It is well. I am just going. I know. It is not true; it is not like that. Thou hast conferred a favor. So also wilt thou be. Anoint thy stomach with mud; scratch thy stomach; twist one leg about the other; [fall] striking thyself on the ground; fall stinking on the ground. There is a stone, a hard stone; strike thy face with it; make the blood spurt forth. Scratch thy nose with the stone,

> or bore a hole with a fire drill into thy windpipe; thou wilt spit [through] there. Just go away; just be an old maid."
>
> But although the words of us men were like this, they were verily only vain, they were verily only weak words. For verily thus the women could torment [young men] into war; thus they moved them; thus the women could prod them into battle.
>
> Indeed we men said:
>
> "Bloody painful are the words of the women; bloody, penetrating are women's words. Indeed we have gone; we have said that we shall not live. Perhaps we shall merit something, O our friend."[18]

Just as the babies were assembled en masse to partake in the public donation of their life force to sustain the ever-thirsty gods, the young girls participated in a citywide spectacle of obeisance to Chicomecoatl, as was the privilege and obligation of all newly pubescent women of Tenochtitlan. It was their first blood that permitted them to participate in the presentation of maize cobs before Chicomecoatl, where they made a mockery of their young male escorts.

The youths' hair was a particular target of derision. Young men wore a long lock that they were permitted to cut only after they had taken their first captive—a powerful incentive for the adolescent who comes of age under the gaze of a community in which his warriorhood, and thereby his manhood, is worn as an external pendant for all the city to see. With the exception of those who were too sick or old, virtually all the men were required to put aside other jobs and commitments to take up the task of soldiering whenever they were called. With the empire's reliance on the redistribution of tribute from conquered states, these conscriptions were not few, and the system of financial rewards and an elevated status for rendering superior military service gave men the chance to move upward in an otherwise unrelenting hierarchy.[19] Since a man's hair conveyed his warrior status, the teasing jousts of women so thoroughly demeaned them that no entreaty for the women to "go off and be old maids" had any hope to restore their maligned dignity. Likewise, the young women's intriguing taunt of "Nowhere hath thy excrement been burned!" referred to the warrior's custom of burning feces on the battlefield, and again called into question their escorts' manhood. While the contemporary reader is perhaps wondering how on earth the Mexica's intrepid warriors managed such an exploit in the heat of battle, this passage makes it resoundingly clear that the young men did not quite measure up; they were not yet like their female counterparts: they had not yet captured blood for the empire.

"Art thou not just a woman like me?" The maiden was referring to the lock of hair that still hung in place. Next, his feeble rejoinder sent her to strike herself and make herself bleed from the impact: "There is a stone, a hard stone; strike thy face with it; make the blood spurt forth. Scratch thy nose with the stone, or bore a hole with a fire drill into thy windpipe; thou wilt spit [through] there." He lamely concluded his retort by saying, "Just be an old maid." With his thin retort, we can discern that the young woman had already given blood for their country, and that his insults were an attempt to lessen her achievement. (Your blood can squirt out any old way. You're not so special. Nyah!) But she *was* special, and she knew it. She was the victorious, blood-winning daughter of the Mexica world that esteemed the red nourishment as the highest possible tribute to the gods.

Menstrual laws that restrict woman's participation in her community's activities are characteristic of a social order that interprets female blood loss as the existence of unclean bodily barriers. All infant males in Tenochtitlan were required to offer blood, and fledgling warrior youths were scorned by the blood-identified group of pubescent women bearing valid claims to superiority. In a society that glorified bloodshed, these examples suggest a cultural disposition that instead of subordinating feminine fecundity, embraced women's reproductive capacity as an admirable aspect of the condition of being female. The ticitl, as the authority on gynecological knowledge, was associated with the ennobled aspects of feminine power. However, the ensuing sections reveal that the masculine principle threatened to supersede this power with the warrior paradigm.

Radical Hysterectomies

So far I have discussed the sexual segmentation of Mexica society and introduced moments in the civic calendar that demonstrate evidence of Mexica vulva envy, meaning that men were inspired by women's ability to issue blood and birth new beings. But envy, as we know, is the most caustic form of flattery. It ultimately led to public contests for the control of women's reproductive capacity. Vulva envy—masculine attitudes that honor and emulate feminine menstruation and birth—offered an extremely limited domain of freedom for womankind. The Mexica Empire constituted a system in which men were better at the creation of humans than women were. Most plainly put, women were demoted once their male counterparts began to bloody the pyramids with their captives and nourish the gods with enemy flesh.

This section examines the beliefs and rites in which males replaced the need for women's wombs in the national project. The "radical hysterectomies" performed by Mexica gods, warriors, and priests convincingly demonstrate that their society gave full rein to the supremacy of the masculine principle. The New Fire ceremony and the myths surrounding the unsuccessful birth reveal the subordination of pregnancy to the function of warriorhood. These examples afford us the context we need to be able to situate women titicih as publicly protecting female agency from its total demonization and usurpation by males.

Although the ancestor of the gods was dual-sexed, it produced an entire pantheon of deities ruled by masculine champions. Ometéotl's segmentation created a schism between forces of light and dark, high and low. Ometéotl had four sons who became lords of the four directions and responsible for activating time and cosmic movement.[20] The Mexica conceived a universe of opposing directions composed of the four natural elements and their ceaseless struggle to vanquish their opposite. Masculine agents governed the four directions and eternally jockeyed for preeminence in a restless roil of aggression.

On the earthly plain, warriors bested women as producers of new humans by providing captives for the city. Describing the profusion of masculine iconography in Tenochtitlan, Elizabeth Brumfiel writes, "Warfare was seen as producing the union of contraries through the incorporation of the defeated by the conquerors; it therefore served as a metaphor for sexual intercourse and fertility."[21] This warrior–captive metaphor for reproduction is seen in several places in the world of ritual. We are told that in the veintena of Tlacaxipeualiztli ("The Flaying of Men"), the populace sent prodigious numbers of captives to die on the pyramids or to perform their last warrior's dance on the gladiatorial stone. In the rites attending a victim's performance on the stone, the captor and captive enacted a peculiarly filial exchange. After the victim was slain by a circle of Mexica warriors, the captor took his blood and placed it on the lips of stone images throughout the ward. Then the body of the captive was divided among the participants to be ingested. Notably, the captor himself would not partake in this ritualized cannibalism, saying, "'Shall I perchance eat my very self?' For when he took [the captive], he had said: 'He is as my beloved son.' And the captive had said: 'He is my beloved father.'"[22] In the tenor and script of this scenario, males eschewed the need for females by achieving a purely androcentric multiplication of the warrior self.

Another androcentric metaphor for the conception of life is found in the New Fire ceremony. Within a culture that dreaded cosmic imbalance during temporal transitions, attitudes toward women during the New Fire ceremony associated the distended womb with the highest kind of treachery, while elevating the roles of male priest and male victim to those of state protectors. The New Fire ceremony was held at the end of a Mexica "century," which lasted fifty-two years. At the end of the old bundle of years, priests ignited a new fire to maintain universal order under the administration of Ometéotl's dominant son. One skilled and careful priest wielding a fire drill sparked a blaze on the chest of a captive and immediately fed the captive's heart to the nascent flame. If the fire did not light, the Mexica believed that demons would descend to eat them. The womb would be implicated in the world's demise, for when night fell, "all were frightened and filled with dread." It was said that if the sacred fire could not be drawn, the sun would be destroyed, eternal darkness would ensue, and "demons of darkness" would descend to eat the flesh of men. Everyone climbed to the tops of their homes to avoid the ground and the house below to await the new fire. Pregnant women donned masks of maguey leaves and were shut into granaries, as it was believed that they "would be changed into fierce beasts."[23]

The New Fire precautions signaled that the womb could turn on the populace at the most vulnerable time in the cycle of the ages, and mothers and wives would become demons, devouring Tenochtitlan's citizens if the sun were to be extinguished. The priests, on the other hand, achieved new life for the state by enacting a crucial performance of symbolic consummation between fire drill and heart, priest and captive. With men providing the most important liturgies for the survival of the state and its people, the spectacle of the distended womb was not something to protect, but rather something from which the world needed protection.

Once men were of age—that is to say, capable of detaining and controlling captives—they turned into the ideal progenitors. Women, who had ascended to warrior parity during their first stirrings of menses, were conferred secondary status when it came to the act of procreation. The myths surrounding the afterlives of warriors and mothers eloquently articulate the Mexica regard for these two vocations. The warrior who died on the battlefield became a spirit that escorted the sun to its highest point, whereas the mother who died in childbirth waited to accompany it to the deep recesses of Mictlan (the underworld). When a woman died giving birth, she was called *mociuaquetzque* (valiant woman). After both sexes completed the four-year privilege of escorting the sun, the men returned to earth as butterflies or as hummingbirds, free and light, possessing the gift of flight, at complete liberty to bask in a world of nectar and flowers. The women warriors, after their four-year tour of duty, came back on the five most ill-omened days of the calendar. Having mutated into the fearsome Ilhuica Cihuapipitlin (Celestial Princesses), or Cihuateteo (goddesses), these women returned to afflict sudden deformity, paralysis, or convulsions among children. Their altars were located at the crossroads, and midwives were their particular devotees. No matter what kind of person she had been in life, any pregnant woman was capable of turning into this destructive force, preying vindictively and remorselessly on the young. Even in death, warriors stood to ascend in rank and esteem commensurate with military achievement, while mothers could only look forward to returning as resentful sylphs to maim the offspring that their neighbors had succeeded in birthing.[24]

By making the pregnant womb the enemy, Tenochtitlan naturalized the subordination of women's kind of warriorhood. Pregnant women would morph into flesh-crazed she-demons in an unsuccessful New Fire ceremony; the "Celestial Princesses" returned to the crossroads to wreak jealous vengeance on the young. In this environment, the womb was believed to harbor uncontrollable, mutinous drives.

This interpretation of Mexica gender accounts for the pubescent glorification of the female condition, when young women were envied by their male counterparts for blossoming on the civic stage as "blood winners," and the subsequent devaluation of women's reproductive contributions once the males assumed the tasks of bloodshed and reproduction, winning captives to be bounced down the pyramid steps after their precious eagle-cactus fruit was harvested and fed to the gods. Priests and warriors had effectively replaced the mother paradigm by replicating the act of reproduction, but doing it in ways that did not imperil the fragile boundaries of human time.

Public Defenders

The midwife-hiring ceremony, birth incantations, and custodianship of the sweat bath (*temescal*) establish the wise woman's elevated status that she enjoyed despite the ascendancy of the warrior paradigm. This last section investigates performances in which titicih were obligated to compete with warriors who attempted to erode the dignity and specificity of womb knowledge. These contests occurred during the laying-away of women who died in childbirth and in the Ochpaniztli veintena. Performances, both constructing and critiquing the complex meaning of gender in the pre-Cortesian setting, functioned as an epistemology, an intellectual system of womb-knowing, that women physicians embodied as public defenders of Mexica feminine knowledge systems.

In a well-to-do household, the seventh or eighth month of gestation was celebrated with an extravagant banquet, at which elder relations of the pregnant woman entreated the midwife to aid in the expedient delivery of their newest family member. An older male relative was the first to request the services of the midwife. Notably, his supplicant posture before a skilled woman illustrates the midwife's merits and distinguished her from the domicile-bound principles typical of the feminine world.

> Ye who are here present, ye who are mothers, ye who are fathers, verily, now, the child, the girl, the maiden, suffereth. For already it is thus. But behold, what hath our lord willed? Perhaps there is death. May ye help her; may ye show her to the sweat bath.

> May she come unto, may she come to know our mother, the grandmother of the baths, Yoalticitl, who adviseth one, who arrayeth one. In her hands we mature, we achieve our merit. May this verily be the time. Place her in the lap, on the shoulders of the wise one, the skilled one, the midwife.[25]

At this point, it was the midwife's turn to deliver a speech, humbling herself before Toci, grandmother of the gods and patroness of physicians, fortune-tellers, magicians, and steam baths as well as the Lady of Discord (as the Culhuacan king Achitometl knew only too well). After she invoked the power of Toci, the family members entreated the midwife to provide help and protection during the time of birth.

> The mother [and] the old women answered the one who spoke. They said:
>
> "Take up thy charge, precious person, godly mother, our progenitress. Aid Ciuhapilli, Quilaztli, and cause the baby, the girl, to go to the *xochicalli* of our lord, the sweat bath, where is to be found, where guardeth the grandmother, the grandmother of the sweat bath, Yoalticitl."
>
> And at once, of her own accord, the midwife fired, heated the sweat bath, where she massaged the pregnant woman's abdomen; she placed aright [the unborn child].[26]

Although women were not granted a space in civic discourse, here we find that the midwife was publicly beseeched to help the parturient mother win a captive for the household. She was the only one intimate enough with the designs of Toci, Cihuacoatl, and Quilaztli to bring about a successful childbirth, and the family members of affluent households employed a duly deferential and reverent tone when requesting her services (fig. 2.1).

The family petitioned the midwife to tend their daughter's temescal, which was a sacred undertaking. The Mexica steam bath served as a symbol for the swelling uterus, with its dark, mysterious properties charged with life-giving heat and moisture. In the Lakota tradition and among other hemispheric American Indian groups today, the sweat bath custom continues to symbolize the return to the womb

Figure 2.1 Mexica midwife as depicted in the Florentine Codex

shelter. Custodians of the lodge heat several rocks over a fire and place them in the middle of the ground within a small hut into which one must enter by crawling. The room is entirely dark, and water is thrown on the stones to generate searing-hot steam. Within its close confines, participants in the sweat lodge ceremony seek spiritual and physical purification. A sweat lodge leader explains that you go into "the womb" and emerge "reborn again."[27]

A place of darkness, the fire of woman meets the steam of man to create life. In this chaotic environment of darkness and heat, new beings are formed. Acting as Toci's agent, the midwife became both priestess and stand-in for Toci, the original "progenitress" (fig. 2.2). Her altar was this place of birth and rebirth, whose womb structure prevented the warrior-organized city from excising its progenitress from the architectural landscape.

When the pains of labor finally appeared, the midwife arrived to bathe the mother in the temescal and administer medicines for a speedy expulsion. The incantation recorded in Ruiz de Alarcón's treatise is

Figure 2.2 Florentine Codex, Ilhuica Cihuapipitlin—Women warriors returned as "Celestial Princesses" to haunt the crossroads

included here in Nahuatl and in English. Along with the ceremonial dialogue at the time of contracting a midwife, its survival over the centuries following the conquest constitutes the only known transmission of the female titicih's voices and thoughts. This glimpse at Mexica versification tells us that women not only commanded sophisticated knowledge of medical practices but also transmitted a corpus of gendered poetics through the practice of oral recitation. The ensuing birth chant suggests the authorial role of women in the world of Mexica incantatory poetry:

tla xihualhuian	Please come forth
macuiltonalleque	Those of the Five Signs.

nonan ce tochtli àquetztimani	My mother 1 Rabbit With Head Upraised:
ye nican ticyocoyaz	Soon you will create here
xoxouhqui coacihuiztli	Blue-green Pain.
tla tiquittacan	Let us see
ac mach tlacatl	Who appears to be the one
in ya nincan techixpolotiuitz	Who is now coming to efface us here.
tla xihuallauh	Please come forth,
tlacuel tèhautl	Well now, you,
tlamacazqui	Priest Nine Crackled;
chicnauhtlatecapinilli	
tla nican ticpehuican	Let us drive out here
in coçauhqui coacihuiztli	The Yellow Pain,
xoxouhqui coaçihuiztli	Blue-green Pain.[28]

Ruiz de Alarcón's treatise tells us that the ticitl addressed the chant to their fingers and the earth. "Those of the Five Signs" denoted the ticitl's own fingers, offering up the merits of her own hands that would wrest the new being from where the god Tezcatlipoca ("Shining Smoke") had seated it within its mother's womb. Tezcatlipoca, patron of sorcerers and the night sky, was also the patron of humans on the earth's surface. That is to say, during the span of time humans walked the terrestrial plane, they were his servants, as he was the giver and remover of life.[29] "1 Rabbit With Head Upraised" referred to the earth's surface, summoning the quintuple manifestations of the feminine earth goddesses to aid in her efforts to seize a captive from darkness. Tobacco, the workhorse of native remedies, is invoked as "Priest Nine Crackled," probably referring to the drying, crushing, and pounding that tobacco plants endured to produce the powdered form used in medicine. After invoking the tobacco, she positioned the laboring woman for birth.

In the event of a delayed or difficult birth, the ticitl burned copal (resin incense) and Mexican mint marigold (*tagetes lucida*) and intoned the following:

nota nahui acatl milintica	My Father 4 Reed Swirling,
tzoncoztli	Yellow Hair;

iztac cihuatzin	White Woman;
coçauhqui tlamacazqui	Yellow Priest.

In this chant, "Father 4 Reed Swirling," "Yellow Hair," and "Yellow Priest" were all names for the motion and colors of the fire that was kindled for the occasion of birth. The incantation for a labor that continued to grow more dangerous for mother and unborn child elicited the following incantation:

tacuel tla xihualhuia	Well now, please come forth
tliliuhqui tlamacazqui	Black Priest; Please go
tla xoconquixtiti in piltzintli	and pull out the little child
in ye quitequipachoa	Which is now troubling
teteo ypiltzin	The child of the gods.
tla xihualhuia	Please come forth,
in tiquato	You who are Quato,
in ticaxoch	You who are Caxoch.

Entreating the medicine ("Black Priest") to release the child from the birth canal's perilous grip, the midwives also called on Quato and Caxoch, two of the Cihuateteo (goddesses) who had perished in childbirth during their human lives.

Possum's tail was the preferred labor inducer, but if labor continued to be impeded, the midwife prayed in earnest to the goddesses Quilaztli, Cihuacóatl, and Toci. Should she fail to expel the child, the parturient woman's family had two options. They could elect to save the mother, in which case the midwife inserted her obsidian knife and withdrew the child in pieces. If the family decided against this course, then the midwife withdrew from the room and enclosed the woman, leaving her to join her child in valiant death. Once life had left her, they bathed her and dressed her in new clothing, with her long, loose hair flowing around her.

Although the Mexica normally burned their dead, a particular ritual surrounded the laying away of these unfortunate women. They were swiftly washed and dressed. Instead of taking them through the front door of the home, a new hole was broken in the back wall, through which they were removed. With an escort of midwives who shouted and brandished shields, the bereaved husband would carry his departed wife to a crossroads to be buried. The group risked attack by young warriors who sought to wrest a fragment of her corpse.

> And the midwives, the old women, assembled to accompany her. They bore their shields; they went shouting, howling, yelling. It is said they went crying, they gave war cries. Those called the youths, those whose task was yet warfare, went encountering them, went skirmishing against them. They went skirmishing against them as they desired to seize the woman. It was not play fighting, not plundering; when they fought, they truly made war.[30]

Fending off the youths, the contingent of midwives took the departed to the crossroads, where they and the husband took turns guarding the body over the course of four days and nights to prevent its theft.

The dead body of a woman who perished in childbirth was a coveted prize. The Mexica believed that a clipping of her hair or one of her fingers would paralyze their enemies on the battlefield. But unseasoned warriors were not their only contenders: "Also the thieves . . . diligently sought the *mociuaquetzqui* [*sic*]. They took her left forearm. They say they bore it with them when they robbed; therewith they caused the members of the household to swoon."[31] A tap on the door from the left forearm of a "valiant woman" was sufficient to paralyze all the householders within, allowing a sorcerer to perform all manners of crimes against property and person. Called "arm dancers" in the *Florentine Codex,* these villains were counted among the most feared and malevolent sorcerers of Tenochtitlan.

It is easy to imagine why the midwives fought to keep their departed charge from the dubious designs of thieving sorcerers, but it is harder to understand why they mounted such a determined defense against the young townsmen who would have used the relics from the woman's remains to achieve success on Tenochtitlan's military campaigns. Like the scathing jibes that so seared the youths during the festival of Chicomecoatl, the tension between the sexes here flared into torment. Unlike the young women who took jocular swipes at the youths' pretensions to manliness, the women healers fought them in earnest, with real shields and battle cries in uncontained hostility. Instead of seizing the opportunity to unite under the banner of

Tenochtitlan's military ascension, the midwives demonstrated an alternate loyalty: they guarded a feminine locus of power from the masculine national project. As the clear Mexica state priority was the engorgement of empire through the subordination of other groups near and far, the midwives' defense of the mociuaquetzque is a notable moment in which solidarity with the feminine principle was prioritized over that of warriorhood and empire. In this laying-away ritual, and most particularly in the defense of the mociuaquetzque remains, we see women healers hold the keys to a weapon so potent as to be coveted by powerful sorcerers and virile youths alike. It was not beyond the tolerance of the Mexica imagination to have decreed the official redistribution of the mociuaquetzque's fingers—the huey tlatoani himself might have collected them for his personal armory and passed them around on feast days amongst his favorites—if the state had deemed it prudent to hurdle the shields and claim the mociuaquetzque for its own campaigns. Yet somehow a clutch of old women was formidable enough to protect the boundaries of the mociuaquetzque's mortal remains. We can conclude from the laying-away ritual that a power center derived of women's fertility was successfully and publicly defended by Tenochtitlan's women physicians, in spite of the aggressions of the city's most feared wizards and able-bodied warriors.

Another ritual in which women titicih formed a united front against the city's warrior paradigm was in the veintena held in honor of Toci. Mexica midwives were central to the eleventh-month veintena called Ochpaniztli, or the "sweeping of the roads" that took place during what is today our calendar month of September. This ceremony held a special place in the Mexica year: it initiated the season of war. The public rites began on the second week of the month; the tenor of its first days was solemn. A procession of four rows of youths danced in rigid formation to the steady beating of a kettledrum. Carrying roughly cut flowers, only their hands moved up and down to the somber percussion (with the exception of the mischievous few who, we are told, lip-synced the drum's cadence while in formation). With great care they repeated this performance from afternoon to sunset over the course of eight consecutive days. Following this period, the pace and mood of Ochpaniztli shifted dramatically.

Some forty days before the veintena, a woman was purchased for the event. Captive for forty days, the first twenty were spent in carefully guarded enclosure. Over the next twenty days, the midwives dressed and adorned her as Toci, leading her through the streets, where she would be hailed and revered as the goddess herself. This ixiptla—a human turned into the living presence of the god—was made to "dance and take pleasure," for if she cried or showed distress, it was believed to provoke many stillbirths and warrior's deaths. Seven days before the festival, seven elderly women physicians came to cheer her and treat her with the utmost care, being sure to compliment and amuse her so that she was as happy as possible.[32]

The eight days of solemn drumming ended when the midwives divided themselves into two separate squadrons and mounted a mock battle, pelting each other with balls of reeds. Their antics were staged for the benefit of their Toci stand-in, the festival's celebrant. She was allowed to make the first attack on the team of rival physicians. They all wore around their waists small gourds full of a medicinal herb, to denote their healer status, and tobacco pouches around their necks. These skirmishes took place over the course of four days, at the conclusion of which the ixiptla was escorted to the marketplace for her ceremonial farewell—she would not be alive to visit it again.

The priests then escorted her back to her house near the temple, and the midwives continued to encourage her, telling her that on that night, the tlatoani—the highest ruler of the empire—would sleep with her. Adorning her with Toci's garb, at midnight they took her in grave silence to the temple where she would die. No sooner did the victim arrive than she was killed and flayed. A naked priest, the tallest and strongest among them, clothed himself immediately in her skin, thereby transforming himself into the new Toci ixiptla. Still cloaked by the night sky, the solemnity gave way to terror as Toci and her contingent of woman physicians chased the assembled warriors through the main precinct with brooms soaked in human blood. The female organs on the strongest of priests, and the sodden brooms, both emblems of essentialized, yet eerily externalized, femininity, caused the city's warriors to flee in real terror.

The next day, the tlatoani distributed regal weapons and accoutrements among his warriors, who then assembled to repeat the dance with which they had initiated Ochpaniztli. This time, instead of flowers, they brandished official arms and shields, and the mothers, wives, sisters, and daughters of Tenochtitlan assembled to mourn in anticipation of the men's deaths on the battlefield. In another squadron of dancers, the midwives danced with Toci, adding now the dramatic accompaniment of their high-pitched voices to the sober kettledrum and the ululations of the nonsacerdotal women.

Ochpaniztli proclaimed the official role of women titicih, enunciating their definitive position on the Mexica civic stage that was populated by warriors, rulers, priests, and domicile-defined womanhood. While normative expressions of femininity included food preparation, cleaning, and the silent weaving and embroidering of fabrics, the woman physicians as a group plainly represented a different kind of force. These took to the streets during the Ochpaniztli ceremony in open defiance of the warrior paradigm, to carve out a civic space for feminine agency. As in the laying-away of mothers who perished in childbirth, the warriors fled in unfeigned terror from this assembly, not because the titicih could outmaneuver them in a contest of brute physical might; what provoked their retreat was the knowledge the titicih could wield. Instead of from a physical threat, they ran from a knowledge system of which the women elders were masters. Every year at Ochpaniztli, titicih reminded rulers, warriors, and priests that they were custodians of a particular locus of power: an awe-inspiring conjunction of medicine and discord, of matronly nurturance and the dangerous fertility that were exclusively female.

Conclusion

Reviewing the life cycle of Mexica womanhood, the early years were characterized by appreciable glimpses of parity. While males were preened to fulfill their destinies on the warpath, early infancy and adolescence were marked by ceremonial occasions that suggest the presence of vulva envy. An examination of Tenochtitlan's veintenas—their major public ceremonies held every twenty days—reveals scenarios in which male infants and adolescents emulated—or envied—the female condition. During "The Great Perforation," priests incised the male infant's genitals but did not take blood from the female infants in this area. On the feast days of Chicomecoatl, the goddess of sustenance, newly menstrual women were accompanied by as yet unblooded warrior youths. If these dared flirt with the young women, they were met with a barrage of diatribes that demeaned their bloodless manhood. The gendered exchange during Chicomecoatl's ceremony tells us that womanhood was acknowledged on the Mexica social stage as a category imbued with intrinsic power.

Although this feminine procreative power was envied by youthful warriors, it was later appropriated by battle-tested men and priests who glorified the warrior principle. Through rituals such as the New Fire ceremony and the beliefs surrounding the afterlives of women who died in childbirth, the balance between male and female merit was tipped in favor of the warrior. Once women left behind early adolescence to assume maternal functions, the warriors and priests overtook them. By capturing and slaying sacrificial victims, the men performed the crucial task of stabilizing cosmic order. The "captives" housed inside the woman's womb were construed as a force for Tenochtitlan's denizens to fear: the pregnant body was a liminal zone between the supernatural and the human, and ultimately feminine fertility bore too much risk to be held in the same high regard as its male counterpart of military conquest.

However, feminine reproductive power was not without its public defenders. The elderly women physicians proved more than a match for the city's warriors on the occasions of the laying-away of women who died in childbirth and the veintena of Ochpaniztli. These scenarios were no mere rehearsals of feminine agency and authority—the city's strongest warriors were driven away in dread by blood-soaked brooms in the hands of aged midwives. Both blood and brooms were emblems of femininity, but these were not brandished in a contest of martial skills. The women titicih repelled throngs of warriors because they were custodians of a Mexica feminine epistemology hewn from the world of empirical and sacred genealogies of knowledge in which men could presume no part.

3

Plotting Prospero's Daughters

LAST YEAR I THOUGHT TO INCORPORATE Women's History Month, celebrated internationally in March, in my Spanish language classroom. I asked first-year college Spanish students to pick a woman in history, and to use their fledgling Spanish-language skills to come up with descriptors of this person without mentioning her name. Because this guessing game is a frequent activity in my language classroom, the students knew what I expected them to do, and set out in small groups of three or four to write their sentences. My standard practice is to go around the classroom while the students are at their initial brainstorming stage and check in with each group to ensure that they understand the instructions and are working on task, and that no two groups are repeating a given subject. At this point I sometimes make suggestions if I find them unable to agree on a person to describe. The first group I observed was working hard to create sentences about Marilyn Monroe. I emphatically put forward that with so many women making important contributions, Monroe was not a choice that did justice to the spirit of the theme. They hunched over their notebooks to feign remorse—a performance to conceal their ambivalence on a topic that seemed to evoke much emotion in their professor. One among them tried to explain that he had made a case for the selection of Harriet Tubman, but none of the others had a clue as to who that was. Apparently, Monroe was the only woman with whom they were universally acquainted. We discussed various options at length, until we finally settled on a different "historical" personage, one who was possibly even more problematic, but whose enduring virtue to me, at that moment, was the fact that she was not Marilyn Monroe. They decided to describe the biblical Eve.

So much time had elapsed working with the first students that I had not visited the other groups to see whom they were describing. The clock had run out, and it was time for them to read their work aloud. I then listened as two different groups read their clues, to reveal that they too had chosen Marilyn Monroe. In other parts of the classroom, a group had picked Jacqueline Kennedy, and one had chosen Mother Teresa, while the final group had described Paris Hilton as its woman in history.

What would have happened if I had asked these college first- and second-year students to discuss Latina women in history? Alarmed by this prospect, I tested the question on a close friend about the Mexican women in history of whom he was aware. To provide a fuller context, this friend, who shall remain nameless, was born and raised in west Texas in a Tejano (Texan Mexican American) family. He was in his mid-thirties and had the benefit of over four years of college education at the time of our conversation. I brought the subject up over lunch at a Chinese restaurant.

"Jessica Alba," was his immediate reply.

"No. You need to give me the names of women in history. Not pop stars or movie stars."

"Flor Silvestre. You know, the wife of Pepe Aguilar."

"Not singers. Women in history."

"Okay. Uh . . . Frida Carlo. You know, the unibrow."

"You mean Frida Kahlo?"

"Yeah, whatever."

"Who else?"

"Hm. Ah! María Sabina."

"Okay. Anyone else?"

When my friend was unable to name any other woman in Mexican history, I asked him about the men. He was able to respond to this question with no hesitation.

"Pancho Villa, Emiliano Zapata, Diego Rivera, Benito Juárez."

He stopped.

"Anyone else? Do you think you can name five?"

"Cantinflas."

"I don't want names of actors."

"Okay. Capitán Márquez . . . you know. From Chiapas."

"Are you talking about Subcomandante Marcos?"

"Yeah, him. . . . Hey, you know what? This isn't fair. I'm hungry for lunch."

I assured him that if ever the interview made it into my study, I would be certain to include this disclaimer.

Experience as an educator tells me that for those who have not specialized in Latin American or women's studies, few women of the Americas in history are noticed. This should not be too surprising: the genre of intellectual biography is antithetical to the mainstream's memory of its female protagonists. Remembered for seduction rather than deduction, the salient female figures are a chop shop of measurements and lusty screen pouts. Biography emphasizes their relationships with men, rather than their contributions to society. Perhaps a Marie Curie or a Simone de Beauvoir are salvaged from the heap of body parts, but Latin America has long normalized the excision of women from its intellectual historiography, with the notable exception of Sor Juana Inés de la Cruz, our rara avis.

In the previous chapter, I showed that intellectual agency of precolumbian Mexica women was most fully embraced in the field of medicine. However, the Hispanization of the New World brought new attitudes about who was allowed to participate in the activity of knowledge production, and how this activity was to be accessed. With the advent of colonization, the region had become host to two different and mutually unintelligible worldviews. Guillermo Bonfil Batalla calls these two civilizing projects "Imaginary Mexico," referring to the European civilizing project, and "Deep Mexico," which denotes the Mesoamerican project that predates, and contradicts, Western imperialist operations. The women inhabiting Mexico's rarefied world of courtly love, social climbing, and solemn seclusion belonged to a different civilizing project than did their indigenous and mestiza counterparts. Given that Imaginary Mexico's women thinkers followed a Europeanized route to the emancipation of intellectual activity, how does an examination of the daughters of the Western elite in the New World make its way into a book about Mesoamerica? I include both Imaginary and Deep Mexico in my study, because both must be interpreted to piece together the full story of women and knowledge in Mesoamerica. Prospero's daughters, the women who constituted the colony's elite norm during the colonial period, represented exemplary femininity in Imaginary Mexico. This chapter historicizes the policies and sentiments that characterized women's acquiescence—and resistance—to patriarchal plots of fathers, husbands, and church confessors. As privileged whites and well-off mestizas, they had more access to literacy and formal education than did the women of Deep Mexico, pioneering the introduction of women into the world of Western theoretical work.

Although the present chapter interrogates the exclusion of women from positions of "legitimate" intellectual authority within the national category, my focus on Mexican citizenship is intended as a representative negotiation between state organization and women's intellectual agency, rather than as a conflation of the Mexican condition and postcolonial Mesoamerica. European philosophy and theology, and later the galvanization around women's rights to learn and participate as thinkers in the public sphere, came into contact with Mesoamerican epistemology in the Americas, resulting in the dichotomy between elite and "underdeveloped" conceptions of knowledge production. Patriarchy segmented society in different ways for different people. Women of the elite were barred from public theoretical work and also from the medical specialization that their Indian and mestiza counterparts pursued. Religiosity, and later education and politics, were the fields in which women were found to circulate a degree of intellectual currency. For these women, national citizenship was public confirmation of intellectual parity. The examination of Mexican political dispositions reveals the route that the Western civilizing project traversed to end up with the present segmentation of women's ways of knowing according to the hierarchies of race, class, and gender that were a legacy of the colonial order.

This chapter's title has several tributaries that must be acknowledged. First, there is Shakespeare's *The Tempest,* in which Prospero is the deposed Duke of Milan who lives with his daughter, Miranda, on an uncharted island surrounded by a wilderness of ocean. Because Prospero and Miranda are attended by Propero's magically enslaved native subjects, the brutish Caliban and the graceful Ariel, seminal Latin American thinkers such as José Enrique Rodó (*Ariel,* 1900), Roberto Fernández Retamar (*Caliban,* 1971), and more recently Junot

Diaz (*The Brief Wondrous Life of Oscar Wao*, 2007) have all mined *The Tempest* as a narrative with insightful metaphors for colonial tyranny. Shakespeare's play has also been visited by feminists interrogating patriarchal hegemony, for Prospero's plot is succinct: the virgin daughter of fifteen is to ensnare a magically shipwrecked prince and resuscitate trampled alliances. Marriage is Miranda's opus, her reason for being and the maximum expression of her value in a patriarchal setting, for it brings her father's plot to fruition. But if Prospero's daughter were to have plots of her own, what would these be? Can we envision a space for Miranda's aspirations that does not reproduce the patriarchal axioms that she has internalized? Additionally, the feminist scholarship of Jean Franco contributes to my examination of "woman" as a national category constructed by those in power for the purpose of political expediency. Franco's *Plotting Women: Gender and Representation in Mexico* (1989) provides a pivotal historiography of Latin American women and authorial agency. Joanna O'Connell's *Prospero's Daughter: The Prose of Rosario Castellanos* is also to be noted for its specific treatment of Rosario Castellanos, a contemporary Mexican woman writer, in light of Shakespeare's metaphor.

To plot Prospero's daughters, I take into account the two major approaches to the history of Latin American women that Asunción Lavrin identifies in *Latin American Women: Historical Perspectives*. The first tendency is to use educational and legal documents as the primary material on which to build theories about social norms. The problem with this body of literature is that it either tells women how to behave or limits its remarks on their activities to the times when they misbehave. This moves the typical feminine life beyond our ken, since most women lived neither as exemplary Christian role models nor as depraved sinners, but rather along a continuum of behaviors and sentiments that encompassed both poles, with the vast majority of their experience falling somewhere in between. The second approach involves the charting of extraordinary cases, in which rigorous bibliography is generated to address the outstanding departures from the norm in history as though these were representative, rather than exceptional, events. Lavrin calls for a "type of work that would allow us to sample the lives of a larger number of women, closer to being more representative of their times and classes."[1] With apologies to Lavrin, this chapter succumbs to both of the tendencies described above and does not offer the type of work that emphasizes representative events or experiences. Here, I mention trials in which women at the margins of New Spanish society were sentenced for their crimes, and cases in which women broke through the barriers of gender to distinguish themselves in public arenas. But the goal here is not to suggest a new model for historicizing the normative feminine experience in the colony or republic, nor is it to gaze at the stellar orbits of its isolated Athenas. There are many conversations on women thinkers in New Spain and Mexico that are limited to the critique of the life and works of Sor Juana Inés de la Cruz, and while my study is considerably indebted to what these studies contributed to our understanding of women's intellectual agency in Mexico, it is also necessary to take a broader historical view that examines the architecture of exclusion. Here, I apply the methods Lavrin describes toward a different end. I plot Prospero's daughters with the goal of interrogating the policies that barred them from the institutions that granted "legitimate" intellectual competencies, and of understanding what kind of theoretical work was available to them given their exclusion from masculinist and elitist philosophical circles.

When looking back in time, it is anachronistic to hunt for a team of Mirandas huddled around the common goal of transmitting a system of knowing. When historicizing Mexican philosophical currents, the customary route tours American manifestations of European movements, like this: Tridentine Catholic beliefs overwhelmed and demonized colonial flirtations with humanism; the Spanish Counter-Reformation employed all possible resources to dim the Enlightenment; notes of French rationalism sneaked in with the Bourbon reforms; the neoclassical winds stirred revolutionary sentiments; Comtean positivism provided the perfect script for white supremacy in the new republic; the embrace of Marxism and socialist ideals contested racist and oligarchic social structures into the twentieth century. That is generally how theoretical work is plotted when it comes to the male sphere, but the daughters, sisters, mothers, wives, and mistresses of Mexican men could seldom hold an audible role in these movements.

Throughout this entire tour of Mexican philosophy, women were not permitted to be civic actors. As disenfranchised denizens, women thinkers were exiles in their own homes. Additionally, in the above scheme of Mexico's thought production, the third world is subordinate to the first. For a feminist space to be detected in the Third World, first it has to be acknowledged that it was widely accepted that their male counterparts are seen as adopting, rather than as generating, the important theoretical work that trickled down from "developed" nations. During its colonial period, the political system sought to expand and enforce the power of the crown and the cross, policing the flow of ideas to those that successfully sedimented Iberian supremacy. After Mexico became a nation, Mexican thought was heavily encumbered by the need to resist the imperialist sentiments of its powerful neighbor to the north, while coming to terms with its cultural and economic heterogeneity. Women were expected to support the project of nation building as defined by the political survival of a country that was not widely acknowledged as having "philosophers" as much as it did "revolutionaries," or cultural innovators, who were seen as heirs to liberal or conservative currents of European origin. For all the opportunities they were granted to come into contact with theoretical currents in such a climate, women were not unlike house slaves or children residing at a frontier outpost. Through these constraints, it is remarkable that some among Prospero's daughters managed to resist the mandate of subordination and invent themselves beyond the patriarchal directive of enclosure.

O Brave New World

What attitudes about gender did Iberian conquerors bring to the New World? Unlike their Mesoamerican counterparts, Iberian women were excluded from the practice of medicine. Before the fourteenth century, healers had been championed by the supreme figure of the Virgin Mary and had long been depicted in medical treatises, hagiographic literature, and Marian works. However, the Valencian statutes of 1329 barred women not only from university study, but also from prescribing medicine. As in the Mexica world, female physicians had not been restricted to the duties of midwifery but had constituted legitimate practitioners in many areas of medicine. When the Western professionalization of the field required university study, women could not legally comply.

Medical historians generally posit three interrelated causes for the professionalization, and thereby the masculinization, of healing: (1) the authority rendered to book and manuscript learning, (2) the rise of universities and their concomitant founding of medical faculties, and (3) the translation of Arabic medical texts into Latin. University training, especially the completion of the four-year *studium generale,* became a common requirement for the licensing of physicians.[2] Entrance into the university system by women was prohibited by law, and although women continued to practice illicitly, they were increasingly persecuted for doing so.[3] By the time the Spanish had turned their gaze westward across the Atlantic, they had already managed to expel women from the practice of medicine, even in the obstetrics field, where their Mexica counterparts enjoyed exclusive authority. Medical specialization was arguably the one arena in which Mexica women performed as fully legitimized intellectual authorities. The Iberian Peninsula, from the age of exploration through the conquest and colonization of New Spain, offered no near analogue.

Although they were not legally sanctioned to perform healing, Iberian women sought and accessed marginal venues for intellectual agency in specific ecclesiastic outlets. The role of the church cannot be overstated in New Spain; no understanding of colonial life can be attempted without an appreciation of this totalizing institution. The fusion of church and state had begun in the fifteenth century when Ferdinand, the king of Aragon, married Isabella, the crowned monarch of the kingdom of Castile. Each hailed from the royal House of Trastámara, the first dynasty to preside over what could properly be called Spain. As major Catholic sovereigns, their alliance brought to a conclusion the seven-centuries-long process of expelling, forcibly converting, or killing their Jewish and Muslim neighbors and subjects, thus securing Spain's position as a world power and forging a Spanish identity that was indistinguishable from that of a Catholic one. Spain's "purification" of its non-Catholic subjects is called the Reconquista, or Reconquest. As the world's most powerful empire, Spain believed it had been divinely appointed to serve as the church's defender and to carry the cross to all antipodes.

At the close of the fifteenth century, the Spanish Empire was poised to begin its hungry expansion westward across the Atlantic as the heralds of Christianity, and the centuries-long fight against non-Christians came with the conquistadors to the New World. Records show that Jews were frequently tried and convicted for retaining their pre-Christian customs in the Americas. Shortly thereafter, Protestantism surfaced as another threat. In response to the Protestant Reformation (1517–1648), one of the important early steps taken by Catholic prelates was the Council of Trent, which convened three times between 1545 and 1563 with the aim of stemming the spread of Protestantism and protecting the orthodoxy of the Catholic Church with regard to such principles as the celibacy of clergy, the invocation of saints, the sacrament of penance (confession), and the veneration of relics. Given the environment of Old World theocratic-political contests, the Spanish colonies in the Americas were not just a place to expand the empire and, ideally, amass untold wealth. They were also an extension of the battlefield in which the institutions of church and state conceived the human individual as a subject-soul, one whose most intimate spiritual behaviors were the test not only of doctrinal obeisance, but of national inclusion as well.

When the Spanish crown established New Spain, the church imported its own ecclesiastic structure from Iberia to detect and discipline wayward subject-souls. The Tribunal of the Holy Office of the Inquisition against Heretical Perversity and Apostasy, known as the Santo Oficio (Holy Office) or Spanish Inquisition, set out to detect and punish two major types of crimes: acts of heresy, or the violation of Catholic doctrine owing to ignorance or contempt, and apostasy, the rejection of the Catholic faith in order to practice a different one.[4] Apostasy was the crime that incurred the severest penalties, and for which Jews who had converted to Christianity (*conversos*) were often haplessly convicted. The population inhabiting the area of Mexico constituted an assortment of peninsular and *criollo* (American-born) subjects, along with non-Iberian Europeans, Africans, mestizos, mulattoes, and an ethnically diverse, massive autochthonous population. In the New World as in the Old, Inquisitorial trials mostly dealt with cases of blasphemy and bigamy, reserving the more sensationalistic trials for dealings with Judaism and crypto-Judaism as well as the threat of *alumbrados*. *Alumbradismo* was perceived as a menace in the sixteenth-century church, as demonstrated by the Edict of Toledo of September 23, 1525, which formulated forty-eight terms in which this spiritual movement was deemed heretical. The terms included the interiorization of Christianity, the ideas of Erasmus and Lutheranism, and a personal relationship with God that rejected the need for church authority or works of mercy.[5]

For the women of New Spain, two means were available through which they could articulate ideations of truth publicly: religious mysticism and rational discourse. Both of these options held tremendous risk, as they were arbitrated by the exacting environment of Tridentine Catholicism. Examples of women's mystical and intellectual explorations show us that when a woman's thinking became exteriorized, she violated the elite Spanish ideal of feminine seclusion and drew attention from the disciplinary apparatus of the Holy Office.

For privileged women, seclusion was a central paradigm. Coming into maturity meant marriage or the convent. Both of these options required a dowry that would provide for her necessities, but if a family could not afford a dowry, the lay option for living a dedicated life of worship was available in the vows of the *beata*. A beata was a woman who pledged varying levels of spiritual engagement, and she could live on her own or in a *beaterio*. In convents and beaterios, the women who practiced strongly emotive, ecstatic, and affective forms of spirituality were widely accepted by Spanish culture in the sixteenth and seventeenth centuries. King Ferdinand himself relied on the counsel of Sor María de Santo Domingo, also called the Beata de Pedrahita, an adored visionary who went into prophetic trances and delivered sermons while under the spell of spiritual ecstasy. Investigated by church authorities, her practices were verified as of a sacred nature. Geraldine McKendrick and Angus MacKay write that women were the most prominent practitioners of this particular form of religious fervor. Sor María de Santo Domingo was one among many woman visionaries whose miracles and prophesies were sought by kings, courtiers, and prelates.[6] McKendrick and MacKay conclude that Franciscan spirituality played a central role in the propagation of the phenomenon of feminine mysticism. The Franciscans valued intuitive and emotional forms of spiritual knowledge over knowledge gleaned from textual study. Theological problems were solved through the emotional, rather than textual, experience of grace. In this hospitable environment, Sor María de Santo Domingo gave sermons under trance to a ready audience.

> Sometimes in her raptures Sor María is accustomed to answering difficult questions about theology, profound problems, matters concerning the Holy Scriptures, things pertaining to our Holy Catholic faith or to good customs, the glory of Paradise, the pains of Hell, Purgatory, and the Holy Sacraments. . . . Thus all who see her and hear her respond think that it is a marvelous thing that a poor, ignorant little woman like Sor María, who was brought up in a village, should respond so well and sometimes better than a Master of Theology or a man of great learning.[7]

Under the thrall of spirit, women such as Sor María de Santo Domingo managed to enter the domain of public discourse with their orthodoxy intact.

In the affective spiritual movement, the Iberian Teresa de Ávila (1515–82) was the exemplary case of the clout women could wield on the path of mysticism. Among her achievements was the reform of the Carmelite order, and, along with Juan de la Cruz, she founded the Discalced Carmelites, adhering to a level of poverty and worldly renunciation that scandalized many of her contemporaries. Although processed by the Holy Office, charges against her were eventually dropped, and she was permitted to continue her work. She founded sixteen convents and authored *Camino de Perfección,* written before 1567, and *El Castillo Interior,* written in 1577, both at the direction of her confessor. Beatified in 1614 and canonized in 1622, Saint Teresa was made a doctor of the church by Pope Paul VI in 1970, making her the first woman to be granted this title. Teresa de Ávila's life and writings are thought to be the most prominent intellectual and spiritual influence on women of the New World, and the Teresian example is credited as the inspiration for the establishment of New Spain's convents and monasteries as well as for setting the gold standard for women's expressive culture within Tridentine orthodoxy.[8]

Because of the qualified toleration of female mystics, feminist theorist Luce Irigaray has argued that mysticism constitutes the only place in Western history in which women could be said to have enjoyed emancipation. But in a militarized ecclesiastic setting, every spiritual activity was met with careful surveillance, and this was compounded for women. Certainly María de Santo Domingo and Teresa de Ávila moved in some of the most powerful religious and political circles of their respective moments, but they were also processed by male ecclesiastic authorities who held the ultimate say about the authenticity of their devotional ecstasies. Writings of mystical women's raptures and revelations were generated only at the behest of father confessors, and, as with Miranda's plot, they served to fulfill the desires of the men in power who regulated in the minutiae their most intimate narratives of body and mind.

The first literary manifestation of New Spain's feminine mystical tradition was the autobiography of Sor María Magdalena, which appeared in 1650 and bore the title *Magdalena, monja profesa del convento del Señor San Jerónimo de la ciudad de México, hija de Domingo de Lorravaquio y de Ysabel Muñoz su legítima mujer*. The volume followed the medieval convention of conserving the memories of an exceptional life to guide and instruct the ensuing generations of nuns. In writings about her ecstasies, Sor María Magdalena calmly depicted the occasion in which the Virgin herself instructed her to pray.[9]

Nuns were often ordered to prepare written accounts of the conscience as a form of confession, an activity that belonged to a Christian tradition associating writing with martyrdom and suffering—the very antithesis of our contemporary designations of autobiography, which is intended to report the contributions of an exceptional individual, not to be an act of penitence or self-effacement in service of the divine.[10] As nuns, these women were committed to a life of abnegation in which self-denial was the order of the day, and their spiritual testimonies were strictly scrutinized for any slackening in their mortifications. For a sister avowed to deny any trace of selfhood, to commit her innermost thoughts and raptures to the page was a dangerous endeavor, as this could constitute evidence of personal ambition or sinful vanity. Prelates required these women to engage in self-representation, but at the same time they exacted the strictest abnegation of personal drives.

Another problem was the reputation of nuns for hypocrisy: everyone knew strong emotions could be faked! Emotive spirituality was the only laboratory in which women could expose thoughts and desires, and this small fishbowl was widely regarded as a container of frauds. According to Elisa Sampson Vera Tudela: "The wide dissemination of the figure of a woman dressed in a nun's habit, which badly conceals her vulpine feet, doing an act of charity, as an icon of hypocrisy of the period shows how popular the conflation of religious dissembling and femininity had become."[11] The Teresian model permitted exceptional women to examine spiritual truth, but this was always subject to the scrutiny of Tridentine law and a male gaze that was eager to accuse them of deception and depravity.

The male clergy in the New World exploited mystical biographies of nuns to help bolster the image of New Spain's elite by promoting the selfless acts and penitent customs of its members. However, New Spain also had its own category for denouncing female mystics whose work fell outside the panoptic of the Holy Office. *Ilusas,* or "deluded women," were often housed in asylums. Records from the Inquisition speak of beatas, nuns, and other women who professed to succumb to divine ecstasies under which they indulged in nondoctrinal behaviors. Jacqueline Holler writes about Marina de San Miguel, a beata at the close of the sixteenth century who provided prayer services for her neighbors in which she went into strange trances. She performed the function of spiritual adviser to laymen who came to her to discuss "matters of God and the spirit."[12] Even members of the clergy visited her home and witnessed her trances. She functioned as a local prophet who was sought for her direct channel of communication with the divine. However, she was eventually denounced and processed by the Inquisition, who discovered she had been acting lasciviously with some of the "spiritual friends" who came to her for counsel. Her report to the inquisitor is one of demonically inspired sexuality, which was a common trope for women being processed in the sixteenth century.

> She came to pollution saying dishonest words, provoking to lewdness, calling by their own and dishonest names many filthy and lascivious things, to which she was inclined by the devil, who appeared to her internally as an angel of light . . . and the said devil appeared to her in the form of Christ . . and asked her to uncover her breasts and to have intercourse with him, and thus for the said fifteen years she has had the said carnal intercourse . . . and seeing that she scorned the married life, highly estimating virginity, the said devil, in the form of Christ as when they paint him resurrected, in the same obscene act, told her: this is the law of matrimony, and it is also pleasing to me, and thou should not scorn it.[13]

"The devil made me do it" was hardly an original plea for women in the Christian tradition, and so Marina was not acquitted. In 1601 the Holy Office made an example of her. She was paraded through the streets of Mexico City, naked from the waist up. A crier called her crimes out to the crowds. She received one hundred lashes and was made to pay a fine of one hundred pesos. She was also to provide service at the Hospital de las Bubas for a ten-year sentence, and she could never again don the white habit of the beata.[14]

Marina's case demonstrates that the pious wimple sometimes provided a refuge for a range of lifestyles and proclivities in which women acted on inner impulses in the name of spiritual ecstasies, free from obligations to their fathers or husbands. However, for both the beatific Teresian and the convicted ilusa, spiritual activity was conducted under the surveillance of a militarized Holy Office. Evinced by the vulpine limbs of the caricatured nun, the popular imagination held that the majority of these mystics were nothing more than great pretenders.

If the mystical imagination was risky, a woman's foray into scientific thought was inherently transgressive. In seventeenth-century New Spain, Sor Juana Inés de la Cruz (1651–95), the prolific "Tenth Muse," made her choice to enter the convent not out of spiritual vocation, but to avoid being governed by a husband: "Given my complete opposition to the idea of marriage, it was the least shocking and most decent thing I could do."[15] Her secular poetry and prose in defense of women's thinking and learning are hailed as the New World's first feminist writing. Her radical departure from the conventions of devotional literature have prompted critics to identify her as the first woman in Mexico's history to move into rationalism, thus becoming her gender's first participant in philosophical, rather than theological, activity as this field is defined by many Western construals of the discipline.

Primero sueño, Sor Juana's most important secular poem, describes a dream state in which the spirit and the body are conceived as discrete entities. The subject's departure from her body gives flight to the androgynous soul, thus enabling it to explore space unburdened by the condition of being female.

> La cual, en tanto, toda convertida
> a su inmaterial sér y esencia bella,
> aquella contemplaba,

participada de alto Sér, centella
que con similitud en sí gozaba;
y juzgándose casi dividida
de aquella que impedida
siempre la tiene, corporal cadena,
que grosera embaraza y torpe impide
el vuelo intelectual con que ya mide
la cuantidad inmensa de la Esfera . . .[16]

[Meanwhile the latter, all intent
on her immaterial being,
that portion of the highest being
in whose likeness in herself she took delight,
she thought herself almost loosed
from that bodily chain,
that always blocks her path,
obstructing crudely and grossly interfering
with the flight of intellect through which she plumbs
the vast immensity of the firmament][17]

Written around 1685 and composed of 975 verses, the poem narrates the pilgrimage of the soul during the body's repose, placing this work within the Western tradition of the soul's voyage that Sor Juana would have inherited through the formulations of Plato and his disciples. In this binary opposition of matter and spirit, the soul is freed from its cumbersome body and is transformed into an exploration of knowledge, conceived as the comprehension of celestial bodies and their choreographies. In *Sor Juana Inés de la Cruz o las trampas de la fe,* Octavio Paz privileges her contribution to the genre of the spiritual voyage: "Because her treatment of the theme differs substantially from that of her predecessors, it can be said that her *First Dream* both prolongs and alters the tradition. . . . The universal significance of her poem—a significance that, strangely, no one has yet understood—rests on this fact."[18] Paz underscores the conceptual innovation of *Primero sueño,* stating, "In Sor Juana's dream, not only is there no demiurge, there is no revelation."[19] Although mystical ecstasies report intimate exchanges with God or raptures with heavenly messengers, Paz points out that *Primero sueño* departs from the axis of Western poetry because it denies an encounter with deity or a spiritual revelation, thus leaving the soul in isolation and moving Mexican letters in the direction of secular humanism. In the last line of her poem, "*el mundo iluminado y yo despierta*," the soul returns abruptly to its female host that is imprisoned by the oppressive constraints with which patriarchal society policed women. By introducing the first-person singular pronoun, the poet identifies the femininity of the poem's narrator/dreamer. For Sabat-Rivers, the significance of her conclusion resides in the faith in womankind that she asserts when she announces the feminine self.[20]

By championing the intelligence of women, Sor Juana stepped outside the relative safety of orthodox religiosity and into hostile territory. She was famously silenced by her confessor, Father Manuel Fernández de Santa Cruz, Bishop of Puebla. In 1690, he published a letter from her that she had penned at his behest. In this letter, she criticizes an important male theologian of her day. Calling it the "Carta atenagórica" ("Letter Worthy of Athena"), he published what she had been led to believe would remain private. The bishop, writing under the name "Sor Filotea," to pose as a fellow nun, published a rebuke of the vanity and sinful pride with which she conducted her intellectual life. The bishop silenced her with this public chastisement. Tragically, she then distanced herself from writing and formal learning; the plot of her father confessor left her with no alternative.

The colony during the eighteenth century is not remembered for having championed innovations in women's philosophical production but is described instead by historians as a time when convents were at the peak of their wealth and political influence. Karen Viera Powers holds that conventual life provided the greatest level of self-determination for New Spain's elite women, likening them to "islands of women" who formed "autonomous, hidden kingdoms."[21]

Certain convents wielded remarkable power in the American colonies. In the absence of banking institutions, convents provided lending services, which made internal conventual politics a matter in which all affluent families of the region held a stake: their financial prospects may have been contingent on a particular abbess's favors. Important families aspired to have at least one of their daughters take up the habit to gain influence within the colony's financing structure. As a testament to the obscene wealth accrued by clergy during this time frame, royal restrictions in 1769 attempted to curb the spectacle of ecclesiastic ostentation by limiting the gifts received and servants employed in monastic settings, even as these were routinely ignored.[22]

By all accounts, women of the elite class in the New World found a home for a number of theological, political, and philosophical pursuits within convent walls. While this space was severely restricted by masculine plots, it was nonetheless the site in which feminine intellect found an opportunity for expansion. Teresian abnegation, the dangerous humanism of the alumbrada, the pursuit of scientific knowledge, the political muscle of the abbess: women of New Spain looked to these arenas as alternatives to marriage, motherhood, and the confines of servile domesticity.

Miranda's Mexico

In the year 1821 Mexico finally secured independence from Philip VII's rule and the Bourbon monarchs, but a devastating period of civil unrest was to mark the next half-century. Mexico struggled to maintain its integrity as a sovereign state in the face of bleak odds. After an eleven-year war of independence, the colonial economy was in shambles. Mining and the business of agriculture dwindled. In 1829, Mexico was again at war with Spain when the Old Country tried to retake its former colony. Texas embarked on its own war of secession and won its independence in 1836; the French invaded in 1838, and the United States invaded in 1846 and seized Mexico's northern territories in 1848. Between 1857 and 1860, the young Mexican nation was embroiled in a devastating civil war called the War of Reform (La Reforma), spearheaded by Benito Juárez, the first Indian to become Mexican head of state. Napoleon III invaded and imposed the Habsburg monarchy's rule in Mexico from 1864 to 1867. Benito Juárez and the liberals defeated the monarchy, and President Benito Juárez went on to serve two more terms (out of five total) from 1867 to 1872.

For women, La Reforma introduced profound changes. It put an end to convent life in Mexico as well as the church-funded *recogimientos* (single-women's shelters), and beaterios. The Ley Lerdo abolished clerical and communal properties, and the Mexican Constitution of 1857 guaranteed many civil and political liberties, including freedom of religion. Single women no longer able to seek community houses or convents were in need of secondary education to make a decent living, but this was unavailable until 1869, when a secondary school was finally opened in Mexico City for women. Many women became domestic servants, seamstresses, cigarette makers, textile workers, and prostitutes.[23] No longer viewed as children in need of protection in the eyes of the law, they were also deprived of adult status, as they were denied equal access to education and civic participation. The right to an education became one of the most pressing hallmarks of early Mexican feminism.

The second half of the nineteenth century saw secular possibilities begin to open to women, particularly in the area of education. An 1867 law made primary education obligatory for all. The illiteracy rate at the time of independence had been 99.5 percent of a population numbering around six million; by 1910, the illiteracy rate had fallen to 78.4 percent despite the increase in population to an estimated fifteen million. By 1895, over half the nation's elementary teaching positions were held by women.[24] In 1887, Matilde P. Montoya became Mexico's first female physician. In 1897 the doors opened to a school for reformed prostitutes. Gradually, educational competency was filling the void left by spirituality as the national venue for women's intellectual participation.

The Porfirio Díaz dictatorship (1876–1910) renewed church authority for a brief period after the Reform's strident anticlericalism. A characteristic of the Díaz regime was the lax implementation of the articles of the constitution that redistributed church holdings. This situation, however, seems not to have benefited convents and their satellite communities such as beaterios and recogimientos in a significant way. In 1877, Díaz created the Dirección de Beneficencia to oversee institutions of social welfare. "Todas estas nuevas disposiciones," writes Josefina Muriel, "no pretendieron ya dar nueva vida a los recogimientos de mujeres. . . . A las delincuentes se les mandó a cárceles y a las demás se les dejó atenidas a sus propias fuerzas . . ."[25] While Díaz aided in the church's surreptitious recovery of property, it seems that women as a social group benefited little from his administration. Once the convents, beaterios, and recogimientos were turned into hospitals and prisons, they would not revert to their former purpose.

Under the Porfiriato, the hacienda (plantation) was the center of Mexican economic activity and the principal instrument for regulating labor power and extracting surplus product for internal and world markets. Land barons and elite clergy members were the bastions of Díaz's power, and by 1910 most Mexican citizens were again landless. The "Pax Porfiriano" enticed foreign investment through swift and total repression of dissenting voices. The archaic system of debt peonage remained unchanged from the end of the eighteenth to the beginning of the twentieth century, while Díaz's adherents, making up 5 percent of the Mexican population, grew extremely wealthy. Workers, intellectuals, and landless Indians swelled the ranks of the Mexican Revolution, a rebellion spearheaded by presidential contender Francisco Madero against the Díaz dictatorship and the neo-*porfirista* Huerta dictatorship. In 1911 the Maderistas expelled Díaz, who fled to Paris, where he died in 1915. Madero was president just fifteen months before his disloyal general Victoriano Huerta killed him. Military victories of the revolutionary forces sent Huerta into exile in the United States. Then, Venustiano Carranza, the self-proclaimed first chief of the Army of the Constitution, took over the national palace when his Constitutionalist Army defeated Huerta in the summer of 1914. His administration saw the creation of the current constitution of Mexico, but he was shot down and killed in Taxacalongtongo, Puebla, in May 1920 when his assailants, followers of General Álvaro Obregón who objected to Carranza's choice of presidential successor, overtook him. Although the war is said to have ended in 1917, the power struggles between Imaginary Mexico and Deep Mexico that culminated in revolution continue to be evident in all areas of Mexican society to this day.

Women from all echelons of society participated in this struggle. Many poor women became "*adelitas*"—female soldiers and camp followers who stood behind, and beside, the men in virtually all areas of military service. Less is said about the theoretical work performed by women during this time. Privileged women, those with access to formal learning, could be found in both anticlerical and Catholic camps in a marked schism that was to characterize the problem of political participation of women for the next several decades.

Although secular-oriented women were less conspicuous than the defenders of Catholic doctrine and clergy, radical feminists with socialist orientations struggled against hierarchies based on both class and gender during the period of the revolution. Hermila Galindo is the most recognized feminist of that era. Born in northern Mexico in

1896, Galindo moved to Mexico City in 1911 and joined the progressive Abraham González Club. Its members named her the orator of the club, and it was she who gave a welcome speech to Carranza after Huerta's fall. Carranza recognized her talent, and she allied herself with his cause by writing newspaper articles and giving speeches before women's groups in praise of Carranza and the revolution, countering the views put forth by Catholic women's groups. Galindo published the profeminist journal *Mujer Moderna*. Ana Macías notes that Hermila Galindo was one of the first feminists to name the church as the "chief obstacle to the promotion of feminism in the country." While Porfirian-era feminists may have privately held this view, they knew that public anticlericalism would do little more than offend public sensibilities and exacerbate the hostilities directed at their cause.[26]

By contributing to the revolutionary cause through speeches and publications, Galindo associated feminism with anticlericalism. However, the majority of women's groups remained loyal to clergy and nonsecular projects.

Carranza's administration saw the culmination of revolutionary beliefs in the famous Constitution of 1917, widely regarded as one of the defining achievements in the evolution of democratic thought in the Americas. Predating the Bolshevik Revolution in Russia, it was the most radical constitution in the Western Hemisphere. It declared that common welfare takes precedence over the rights of the individual; promised an eight-hour workday, control of wages, and the end of child labor; and provided the right to organize freely and to strike. It reinvigorated the Juárez reforms by declaring temples of worship to be the property of the state and prohibited the purchase of Mexican territory by foreign parties.

At the Constitutional Convention at Querétaro, most delegates held that women were unswerving religious zealots that, given the opportunity, would retard all strides the revolutionaries had taken to ensure the rights of the urban and rural poor. The group was made up of delegates from all parts of the republic, and from different economic, geographic, and ethnic backgrounds. With Article 130, delegates determined that marriage was a civil contract and reinforced government control of church buildings. E. V. Niemeyer Jr. calls the congress at Querétaro the "apogee of anticlericalism" and points out that hostility toward ecclesiastical authority had grown more fervent in the time between the Constitution of 1857 and its revision in 1917. While Article 123 of the Constitution of 1857 had put federal authorities in control of all matters of religious worship and ecclesiastical forms, Article 130 contained new provisions that further limited clerical activity, making it the most anticlerical constitution in Mexican history.[27] Women received much of the blame for the sway nonsecular authority held in Mexican homes. In the debates, Modesto González Galindo, delegate from Tlaxcala, exhorted his colleagues "to snatch 'the woman from the confessional,' since women were the instrument by which the Church achieved its political objectives and the clergy 'stripped the home of its honor.'"[28]

Women's activism was a ready source of derision at the Constitutional Congress. According to Shirlene Soto, "during the Constitutional Congress, delegates debating the issue of church-controlled education received a message from women in Monterrey protesting anti-clerical measures as 'oppressive of God and our holy religion.' The delegates hooted and roared with laughter when the message was read."[29] On December 25, 1917, Catholics in the states of Mexico, Puebla, and Michoacán published a signed pamphlet protesting federal restrictions on religious education. Tellingly, more than 80 percent of the signatures belonged to women. The men's laughter in Querétaro demonstrates their disregard for the complexity of women's political participation in Mexico.

With the revolution uprooting traditional gender norms, liberals and conservatives each offered their own solution to the problem of modern Mexican womanhood. Informed by socialist ideology, liberals prioritized class struggle but lacked a critique of the patriarchal institutions that had barred women from coming into class-consciousness through education and civic participation. With few exceptions, they refused to acknowledge their own collusion in women's alienation from liberalizing projects. Conservatives, initially opposed to women's civic engagement, soon saw they could draw on popular religiosity for their own agenda and supported women's social action.

The feud between liberals and conservatives was no mere matter of collegial banter over prevailing views: lives were at stake. The Cristero Rebellion (1926–29) proved that both sides were capable of committing deplorable crimes over the church–state conflict. The Cristero Rebellion began in July of 1926, when bishops suspended religious services to protest federal anticlericalism. A popular revolt ensued, with strongholds in Western and Southern states. At the height of the conflict, rebel ranks were some fifty thousand strong. The Cristeros (Catholic guerrilla fighters) were mainly the rural poor, and both church and political leaders were dismayed by the uprising. In June of 1926, President Plutarco Elías Calles ordered the dispersal of every convent in the Republic in a piece of anticlerical legislation unofficially known as the Calles Law. Acting with impunity, government agents seized, deported, assassinated, and even raped women of the cloth.[30] Cristeros, in turn, were responsible for the slaughter of rural schoolteachers, the majority of whom were women. In one incident, not unlike others that took place in Cristero strongholds, a young teacher fled her classroom when she detected a group of approaching horsemen. They lassoed her and dragged her feet first for miles until there was scarcely anything left for her loved ones to bury. In retaliation, government forces took hostages, raided villages suspected of harboring rebels, and looted the countryside.[31] In 1928 Lázaro Cárdenas became governor of Michuacan, one of the states with a strong Cristero following. By 1929 his diplomacy had helped forge a tenuous peace between church authorities and agrarian socialists. Women had been some of the most ardent supporters of the Cristero cause, even though, since they also served as rural schoolteachers, they constituted some of the most vulnerable members of the liberal cause as well.

The church–state conflict and its subsequent co-identification of women and fanaticism continued to define party views well past the Cristero Rebellion. Consolidation of Mexico's modern political party system dates to 1929, when President Plutarco Elías Calles founded the Partido Nacional Revolucionario (PNR). The PNR began making overtures toward women in recognition of their capacity to organize, but, as Jocelyn Olcott points out, the measures to recognize women in nondomestic roles were made "more out of fear than a commitment to justice." In September of 1930, all state governments were required to submit names of organizations that included women. The lists were dominated by Catholic and temperance groups, along with a few labor unions. Communist party organizations did not figure on any of the lists.[32] To be sure, feminist organizers cogently problematized the systematic exclusion of women from progressive organizations. They recognized that it was difficult to engage women in the socialist cause when church-based charities, vocational classes, and traditional support networks had so long offered opportunities to thrive, while masculinist government had provided them no imagination or incentives for enlisting in nonsecular activities. On the ground organizers Concha Michel and Dolores Heduán de Rueda acknowledged the absurdity of the liberal program when compared to the successes of popular religion. Concha Michel declared, "It is completely absurd to arrive in places that have been subject to a religious education saying that 'God is a phantasm and the saints are the products of the fantasies of unscrupulous artists.'" She argued for the provision of practical instruction on the struggle for land rights, improved wages, and drinking water. It was also crucial to address spiritual needs by acknowledging indigenous views to contest the practical cosmogony of the Catholic Church. Heduán de Rueda explained that women's fanaticism was attributable to the fact that "nobody . . . admitted the complete collaboration of the feminine sex as much as the propagators of religious dogma; no door was opened as wide to woman as the door of the religious temples."[33]

PNR leadership encouraged the formation of the female suffragist Ejército de Mujeres Campesinas (Army of Rural Women), to be led by Professor Jovita Boone de Cortina. Voting rights for women existed in many European countries, the United States, Chile, and Ecuador. Although they supported the PNR, the Ejército de Mujeres Campesinas called attention to the party's complicity in reifying gender hierarchies and labor oppression in their own homes. "We consider ineffective . . . the revolutionary efforts of men who now fight to transform a social environment that maintains archaic Roman norms while they keep women, children, and above all the home within the absolute, oppressive, and absurd regime of archaic Roman laws stuck thousands of years in the past."[34] Hoping to win women's loyalty to the national party, the Ejército de Mujeres Campesinas was expected to continue the tradition of feminine abnegation that the party set for them, which amounted to an "ejército" of demure wives, selfless caregivers of the young and the old, and providers of hot tortillas. Women who had helped make the revolution as fearless warriors and camp caregivers to gain rights for the poor were now sent back to the home, where they were to provide compulsory and unpaid work in perpetuity without the status of citizens in the country of their birth. In the name of a fight against the enemies of the revolution, women were not conferred voting rights, ostensibly owing to the division women would produce among the interests of the ruling organizations.

Despite the revolutionary discourse of the day, it was not religious conservatism, but rather misogyny, that postponed women's political enfranchisement between the 1930s and the 1950s. In Mexico, military coups, assassinations, corruption, and dictatorship defined national politics. Women's spiritual proclivities had not been the reason, but rather the excuse, employed by liberals to distance women from the electoral urn. However, despite the absence of a noncorrupt, national electoral politics, voting held the symbolic power to legitimize political actors and validate national participation. The suffrage struggle tells us about the revolution's recasting of gender and national inclusion that brought Mexico into the modern era. The male-dominant political culture, by refusing to reconcile the many ways in which popular religiosity had provided women with a model of agency and a social identity for over four centuries in the development of a nation, sedimented its own hegemony by refusing to integrate any women's organization that did not embrace the postrevolutionary corporatist regime.

Reactionary religiosity was not the only factor in the postponement of women's voting rights, but rather one out of a variety of issues wielded by the congress to kill debate. Postrevolutionary statesmen underscored the example of the Spanish Civil War, noting that when Spanish women voted for the first time in 1933, the Spanish socialist party suffered serious losses. Additionally, differences across women's organizations complicated their proposals before congressional authority, amounting to a multifaceted reconsideration of gender ideologies capable of destabilizing the party's gains. But most critically, the voting process itself was no guarantee of individual participation in a postrevolutionary environment that placed national political and economic survival before the labor and agrarian constituencies that had prevailed during the drafting of the constitution. The increased strength of fascist governments in Europe, worldwide depression, Cárdenas's expropriation of oil, and the outbreak of World War II undercut not only women's progressive campaigns, but the entire socialistic direction of Cárdenas's government.[35] The radical proposals for reform for which Cárdenas is remembered were housed within a corporatist framework that had institutionalized—rather than actualized—revolutionary ambitions.

The conferral of voting privileges on women of all creeds and affiliations ran the risk of exposing the fact that voting had not become a democratic process at all. As a social group, women needed to *seem* more liberal before they could be enfranchised. Cárdenas rebuilt the PRN under the new name of the Partido de la Revolución Mexicana (PRM) in an effort to amplify party participation and settle disputes that threatened to explode into further armed rebellions. Popular participation was sacrificed, and the election of Cárdenas's successor was manipulated to ensure the PRM's rule. By embracing the corporatist framework, the revolutionaries determined that their own objectives took primacy over the principles for which they had fought. In January 1946, Cárdenas's successor, Manuel Ávila Camacho, helped dissolve the PRM and provided the name for the dominant party's next incarnation. This last nomenclature—the Partido Revolucionario Institucional (Institutional Revolutionary Party—PRI) makes it clear that the revolution had grown into a matrix of corporate relations, completely excising the words *nation* and *Mexico*.

With the ensuing presidency of Miguel Alemán, ideals of the revolution were further tokenized until they were no more than a propaganda tool. In a "chivalrous" moment (devoid of any real commitment to justice), Alemán proposed an amendment allowing women to vote in municipal elections. The amendment passed with the overwhelming majority of votes; only the ultraconservative Partido de Acción Nacional (National Action Party) dissented, arguing that female suffrage would destroy the home and derail masculine privileges.[36]

In October 1953, the congress passed the amendment that finally granted women the right to vote in national elections. Feminist historians note that by this time the PRI, Mexico's one-party dictatorship that would rule for over seventy years, had vanquished all memory of egalitarianism and political pluralism for which the revolution had been fought. Just when the vote meant the least, congressional authority deemed it would not be contraindicated to let women share in it. The PRI may have offered a very contingent form of political participation when it conceded the vote, but, for the long battle that had been waged by feminist combatants, it was a promising step.

Conclusion

After colonization, Mesoamerica became the site of two distinct and mutually civilizing projects. Following Guillermo Bonfil Batalla, I refer to these as Imaginary Mexico (Western imperialism) and Deep Mexico (indigenous cohesion). As these spheres produced different categories of womanhood, this chapter examines women's actualization within the first (Imaginary) category but does not delve into the second (Deep). The daughters of landed aristocrats and other Western actors provide the story of women's eventual inclusion in the institutions granting legitimate intellectual competencies.

History tells us that the Catholic Church provided a space in which women could externalize a qualified level of intellectual authority. However, once Mexican society was secularized, liberalizing actors indicted what had once been considered a feminine virtue. Beginning with La Reforma in the nineteenth century, full enfranchisement was denied women on the basis of their perceived religious fanaticism. I have argued that misogyny, rather than religious fervor, was the reason for women's dismissal from political participation. Ignoring the need the church had addressed by providing a space for women's expressive culture, community leadership, and spiritual transcendence, the new leaders of the Republic used female religiosity as an excuse to discredit their civic engagement. Only when electoral power had been thoroughly subdued and the aims of the Revolution of 1910 had become little more than nostalgic slogans did the political party grant women the right to vote in their own country, a concession that legitimized women as political actors without conferring authentic agency. Even so, this occasion marked a victory for the many generations of women that had long decried their exclusion from the national project: they were finally permitted a forum to express their ideas about the Mexican condition.

4

Survivor Woman

From the Inuit in Alaska he learned to survive in the High Arctic and from the Waorani tribe in the jungles of Ecuador, Stroud learned to hunt naked with a blowgun. "How cool is that?"[1]

THE POPULAR CANADIAN-PRODUCED television program *Survivorman* was aired on the Discovery Channel and the Science Channel in 2004, 2007, and 2008. The show's premise was the star's ability to face the elements in the most remote and hostile reaches of the planet, relying solely on his survival skills and knowledge of the local flora and fauna to make it through seven days alone in the wilderness with no food or water and nothing but a few minimal tools. Aside from his Leatherman multitool, his hefty camera equipment, and an emergency satellite phone, his survival implements were usually such everyday items as a few ballpoint pens, a can of soda, and the clothes on his back. The knowledge needed to brave the remote and inhospitable regions of the globe could not be gleaned from the survival course offered through the local adventure shop (which is where the survivalist met his wife). For the thorough understanding of a locale's terrain, Stroud interviewed local indigenous people, such as the Inuit and the Waorani mentioned above.

Easily dismissed by the viewing public is the reality behind the reality show: for each of Survivorman's stints in the unforgiving wilderness, there is a population of local people with scant access to food or clean water, and they live this way not for television ratings or entertainment value, but because this is their home. With this programming, not the indigenous inclination to maintain equilibrium with nature, but the Anglo man's tenacity in battling it, is what gets framed by the camera lens for a Western viewing public.

This reluctance to appreciate the native cultural economy is as old as the conquest of the Americas. Acting as intermediaries between the human plane and the ecological one, Mesoamerican healers have been largely overlooked by Christian catechizers and biomedical doctors. Their deep identification with nature reads, to the Western optic, as an invisible peopling of the Americas that stirs in the background, while the Anglo's narrative takes precedence. Just as environmental balance is undervalued by Western philosophy, so too are systems of beliefs that maintain harmony with the natural world. With disequilibrium established as the normative order, the Western audience is well qualified to dismiss as nondiegetic the voices of peoples that live in ecological equilibrium.[2] Because the achievements of native denizens are not discernible on the Western grid of meaning, Survivorman becomes the Tarzan or the Elvis who imitates the Third World and, through the act of imitation, becomes its superhero.

Mesoamerican Indians have managed to preserve knowledge of local flora and fauna despite the apocalypse of colonization, and preconquest methods of traditional practitioners still constitute a significant part of the health sector. Recent estimates indicate that from fifteen to twenty million of the current Mexican populace seek traditional healing practices from a reported 180,000 recognized practitioners, and this is not to mention the occasional adherents who supplement biomedical treatments with traditional practices.[3] The widespread devotion to these ancient hemispheric forms tells us that the transmission of Indian medical knowledge persisted despite colonial efforts to supplant or defame native epistemologies. This chapter demonstrates that Mesoamerican care continues to be an important part of North and Central America's health sector, despite the Western pressures to control or eradicate indigenous conceptions of medicine and ignore or excise the significance of women specialists in this arena.

Survival of Mesoamerican Medicine

How did traditional healing survive the conquest? Various factors contributed to the persistence of native curatives that are considered in this section. The Spanish, and later the infrastructures of the emerging republics, were ill equipped to care for the autochthonous majority, so European health systems were underrepresented in rural regions. Along with the limitations of resources, notions of race impeded the integration of methods, concepts, and delivery: Europeans believed Indians possessed completely unique physiologies and were thus unable to respond to Western treatments. Additionally, the lack of intercultural dialogue distanced traditional practitioners from Western knowledge systems, as Iberian institutions insisted on the exclusion of both Indians and women from its degree-granting academies. And finally, the survival of native medicine can be attributed to its efficacy. From the earliest days of the colony, Spanish subjects were successfully cured by Indian doctors, and today's advancements have not slowed the stream of international clientele who seek out accomplished Mesoamerican healers to combat chronic conditions for which there are yet no known biomedical cures. By recognizing the attitudes that have impeded the survival of Mesoamerican medicine in the modern age, we are better equipped to envision a social order that restores the important role native thought will play in creating ecologically and intellectually diverse Americas.

Since volumes on ethnobotany, traditional curatives, and regional practices are numerous, this chapter does not attempt to deal with specific diagnoses and treatments. However, because Western and Mesoamerican conceptions of illness are so dissimilar, an overview of the postconquest Mesoamerican disease load is required to contextualize the status of its health specialists.

For instance, a prevalent, pan-Mesoamerican ailment cured by indigenous healers would never be regarded as such by the Western medical establishment. *Envidia* belongs to a family of illnesses potentially related to sorcery. Although it translates to English as "envy," the spiritual implications of envidia go far beyond its Western connotation. Envy and ambition—energies born of egoistic drives—are viewed as corruptions of the healthy being. What I describe as "centripetal" behaviors—ones that promote individual accumulations of property and importance—fall into the sin/pathology category. It is a pan-Mesoamerican belief that individualistic and egoistic drives can stir harmful intentions, while "centrifugal" drives, those that flow away from the individual in the direction of the people in her or his care, are most highly rewarded with the approbation and respect of community members. An example of this social organization is found in the *cargo,* or fiesta, system. Revolving offices, called *cargos*, are held by individuals active in religious and civic life. On the feast days of specific saints, the person who holds the cargo is generally required to incur the cost of the celebration. This considerable responsibility and expense will be assigned only to the most esteemed representatives of the village. Those accorded the highest ranks are also required to give the most back by inviting the entire community to dine at their table, thereby redistributing the benefits of their success.

Another medical complaint rooted in excessive individuation and desire is found in *mal de ojo,* an illness produced by extreme admiration. Babies are most prone to this illness, as even the kindest observers can unintentionally cause the child to suffer. Charms work against ojo, and touching the child can help reduce the chances of causing it harm.

Susto and *espanto* are supernatural forms of shock. A severe fright can result in a person's soul escaping from the physical boundaries of the body and possibly becoming trapped by a nearby spirit being. With espanto, the soul is said to be wandering far away and is maybe too distant to respond to a healer's entreaties for it to return. *Caída de mollera* (fallen fontanelle) is an illness that affects infants and is believed to be caused by a fall from the bed or crib, or from its being pulled away from the mother's breast too abruptly while nursing. *Empacho* (digestive illness) is thought to come from eating too quickly or from the improper combination of hot and cold foods.[4]

The above list serves to demonstrate that a range of illnesses go unrecognized by the formal medical profession but are prevalent among traditional Mesoamerican groups. These ailments may be seen as superstitions by practitioners unaware of an ancient system of beliefs that inform perceptions of health and pathology. For this reason, Mesoamerican healers are crucial to the delivery of a type of care that is respectful of millennial native cosmology and the centrality of community relationships to the conception of wellness, and cognizant of the trajectory of colonization and its impact on care delivery.

Along with an examination of Mesoamerican methods, this chapter discusses the presence of Western medicine and biomedicine in the Americas. Western medicine refers to the theories and practices generated by the Western civilizing project over the centuries of colonial and postcolonial preservation of European hegemony. Biomedicine, on the other hand, specifically refers to the methods and priorities of clinical research and is largely driven by corporate interests and political expediency.

Economic Deficiency

Medical anthropologists studying the colonial period recognize that Spanish tolerance of Indian medical knowledge was partly attributable to the weakness of New Spain's administration. Unable to extend its influence over a vast and diverse newly conquered terrain, Spanish doctors were consulted by Spanish patients, and Indian medicine was tolerated for reasons of lack of resources, rather than ideological accord. According to Noemi Quesada, the chief factor that allowed Mesoamerican healing to survive the austerity of the Tridentine ecclesiastic environment was the limitations of the colonies' infrastructure (1991).[5]

Because religion and medicine were not yet discrete categories at the time of conquest, converting Native Americans to Christianity and administering health care provided similar logistical challenges to the colonial regime. The matter of converting Indians originally fell within the jurisdiction of the Holy Office, but it was soon removed.[6] When fray Juan de Zumárraga's bishopry in 1527 led to the controversial 1539 execution of don Carlos Chichimecatecuhtli, a prominent native nobleman, the Inquisition in New Spain withdrew from the business of burning Indians at the stake and returned to the regulation of its non-Indian population. Philip II formally removed Indians from the jurisdiction of the Holy Office in 1571, not because public burnings of heretics, the parading of offenders in penitential garb, or the ostracizing of apostates had been less than humane, but because the Indian populace had no context for understanding these disciplinary technologies.[7] Thus, native Mesoamerican ritual, probably conserved by about 75 to 80 percent of the populace, would have been expressly exempt from the pages of the Spanish Inquisition. Without the apparatus of an effective state-level tribunal to disrupt Indian knowledge transmissions, Iberian America was limited to the policing of its own kind. Iberian and Mesoamerican healing became segregated from the time of the colony's earliest days due to the practical impossibility of an elite minority policing a diverse, indigenous majority with any meaningful level of scrutiny.

Even for criollos and mestizos at the top of the social pyramid, resources allocated to medical advancement were in short supply. Biomedical research was not to receive full backing in Mexico until after 1938. Before that time, isolated amateurs explored clinical research in small numbers, and medical research, as an organized profession, did not exist until 1939, when state funding began to fuel medical experimentation. It was in 1949 that, under the presidency of Miguel Alemán, the National Indigenist Institute (Instituto Nacional Indigenista—INI) was established to fulfill the Mexican Revolution's promise of equality among its Indian populace. Conceiving health as a human right, its goal was to integrate indigenous subjects into the national project and eliminate the injustices occasioned by conquest and colonization that had not been addressed by the rhetoric of democracy. Not surprisingly, INI considered the primary problem of indigenous groups to be one of an economic nature and proposed solutions such as industrialization and technical innovation. It stood to reason that with modern resources and the democratization of education, the disenfranchised Indian groups would warm to Western methods, and INI sponsored clinics and training programs that would work to promote hygienic practices and referrals to clinics or hospitals. In Guatemala, the Ministry of Health has offered training programs to heighten traditional practitioners' knowledge of risk factors and to decrease maternal and infant mortality rates.[8] In these regions, the ravages of poverty and underdevelopment were blamed for the persistence of traditional medicine, which was perceived as the symptom of an ailing national health sector.

In sum, the economic explanation for the survival of Mesoamerican medicine allows that the colonial environment tolerated native curatives because the Spanish were unable to police the autochthonous population with the same strategies that it used to regulate its Iberian minority. In the contemporary era, the paucity of biomedical initiatives such as local clinics and training programs in isolated Mesoamerican communities is seen as proof of the lack of financial resources. Perseverance of traditional medicine owing to this isolation can be reasoned by economic explanation, and the introduction of biomedicine to all indigenous cultures is perceived as the imperative of a modern, liberal Western state.

Perceptions of Race

Although Philip II had excluded Indians from the jurisdiction of the Holy Office, inquisitorial authorities still received denunciations of Indian healers. After hearing a delation, the court had to make a determination about the race of the accused. Was the accused party fully Indian or of mixed parentage? Racial designation determined whether or not the accused was exempt from tribunal proceedings. The Holy Office received seventy-one accusations against and denunciations of folk healers. Only one practitioner had to succumb to an auto-da-fé—a public act that involved a Catholic mass, a public procession of the guilty party, and a reading of their crimes and sentences. Additionally, the records indicate that only one traditional healer was punished with exile. The majority of the denounced healers were either mildly reprimanded or summarily dismissed, because they carried mostly "Indian blood."

Augustina Rangel was a *castiza* (reportedly three-quarters Spanish and one-quarter Indian) convicted in 1685 of alumbradismo, sorcery, and unorthodox healing practices. Rangel was forced to take an oath abjuring all future medical practice. In 1733, the mulatta María Concepción "La Salvatierreña" was charged with and convicted of providing "malefic" curatives. She received twenty-five lashes and was sent to prison for her deeds. Manuela Rivera "La Lucera" was a castiza convicted of unorthodox healing practices and imprisoned for five years, paraded in 1734 before the city, and given twenty-five lashes at the pillory. These women were reprimanded for the use of hallucinogens, illegal idols and relics during healing rituals, incantations, and using divination to diagnose and prognosticate.

The mystical call to heal was not unusual in the Spanish world, and so in the New World, the problem was not that women mystics cured, but rather their use of precolumbian techniques that enraged ecclesiastical officials. Owing to their mixed heritage, women like Agustina Rangel, María Concepción, and Manuela Rivera were not "Indian" enough to fall outside Iberian jurisdiction, and they had to answer to medical laws befitting their racial status. As long as whites were cured in Spanish ways, and mixed people assimilated to white ways, the Indians were free to heal—or die—in the manner that best pleased them.

Ideas about race were also implied in one of the conquest's greatest paradoxes: the European disease load may have collaborated with the perseverance of Indian methods. The pandemics faced by Mesoamericans during the first centuries of the colony occasioned what can only be described as a holocaust. It is not disputed that from the early voyages of Columbus, Indians came into contact with European diseases to which they had little or no resistance. Most historians concur that European sickness was far and away the greatest killer of the native populations after contact. The size of native populations and their rapid declines after conquest differ greatly, but demographers recognize that Old World illnesses devastated the Pacific and American peoples who had been isolated from Old World pathogens and thus had not developed the immunities needed to cope with exposure. William M. Denevan details the outbreak of European diseases in his study of native populations before European exploration. Strains of smallpox, chicken pox, whooping cough, measles, bubonic plague, typhus, diphtheria, amoebic dysentery, and influenza disembarked along with people and livestock from the crowded Spanish fleets. Historians tend to insert a note here about syphilis being a Native American contribution to the European disease load, not as an overture to balance the tally sheet, but to show that epidemics passed back and forth between both groups. The native death rate was abetted by the activities of conquest in the form of forced labor, the erosion of traditional agricultural systems resulting in famine, the slowing of reproduction, the banning of hygienic practices such as steam baths and circumcision that were associated with pre-Hispanic religious observances, and other causes of suffering and dying imposed by the violence of conquest.[9]

The rate at which indigenous groups succumbed to death from exposure to the biohazard that was European occupation is unknown, but a chorus of demographers remark that it is likely to constitute the most significant demographic tragedy in the history of humankind. One recent estimate of the native population of all Latin America places the count at eighteen million, with about one million in the United States. Henry F. Dobyns, a respected hemispheric demographer, submits that the population of indigenous Americans decreased by 95 percent once the Europeans arrived.[10] However, the debate over how many people populated the Americas before European occupation, or the size of the decline once contact was initiated, is not the locus of this study. What we do need to take from the demographic information is the fact that Indians manifested a wholly unique response to the ailments of the colonizers. And this difference encouraged the idea that Europeans and Indians were possessed of wholly incompatible physiologies.

The devastation of the population influenced both autochthonous and exogenous notions of race. Under the new regime, Indian doctors more readily adapted European medical information when they were forced to cope with previously unknown pandemics. Healing traditions that relied on spiritual explanations may have hastened a group's conversion to Christian beliefs when native gods failed to stave off the onslaught of the bio-weaponry of the European presence. Officials witnessing (and contributing to) these early death waves sponsored the demarcation of Indian and Iberian medical institutions, so there was little impetus for reconciliation of traditional curatives and Western ones.

Not only was European medicine reserved for criollo and mestizo patients, but medicine as a professional pursuit was restricted to the wealthy whites of New Spanish society. "Limpieza de sangre" (purity of blood) did not exclude José Mariano Martínez Peredo from taking years of coursework, but it did exclude him from being able to sit his professional examination in 1778. His physical appearance, and three witnesses from the neighborhood where he was born and raised, testified that he was the mixed-blood child of a priest and his "mulatta" servant. The product of such a union, write Luz María Hernández Sáenz and George M. Foster, could never enter any respectable profession.[11] The prestige of a university degree was conferred only on Spanish and criollo candidates who could document their family's ancestral obeisance to Tridentine religiosity and an unblemished racial pedigree.

Race and class were tightly interlaced in postconquest society. The conferral of medical degrees, Hernández Sáenz and Foster point out, was limited to the elite. *Pompa,* the licenciado (bachelor's) ceremony, involved a procession through city streets to the cathedral where the degree was officially granted. The doctor of medicine had to pay for a much more elaborate rite. A more populous and ornate cavalcade had to be commissioned, along with musicians and a mass at the cathedral. Additionally, a set fee was to be paid to all university graduates and faculty in attendance.[12] That skin color was also a part of this elaborate performance of epistemic exclusivity was a strategy in the sedimentation of Spanish hegemony. The exclusion of indigenous people from elite medical institutions contributed to the sharp delineation between Mesoamerican and Western health delivery that continues to be overt and pervasive to the present day.

Cultural Programming

Although it was accepted that Indians should tend to Indians and have separate ways of healing, these were not to be considered a viable alternative to Spanish medicine. In *Ticiotl: Conceptos médicos de los antiguos mexicanos* (1997), Carlos Viesca discusses Spanish colonial doctors' disdain for Mesoamerican medical knowledge. In 1570, Emperor Philip II sent his personal physician, the naturalist Francisco Hernández, to create an inventory of Mexico's natural history. Over the course of the next seven years until his return to Spain, Hernández described more than three thousand native plants. To nearly all of these plants he ascribed humoral values, which were the official theoretical model in elite Spanish medicine, thereby excluding indigenous explanations of the virtues of their own pharmacology.[13]

At the time of conquest, and for several centuries after, European medicine was informed by Greek humoral pathology, as presented in the Hippocratic Corpus dating back to the fifth century BCE. Galen, born in the Greek city of Pergamon around 125CE, wrote extensively on Hippocrates, whose humoral theories dominated Western medical thought for the next sixteen centuries and were largely uncontested in the Spanish context at the time of American colonization. Four humors—these being black bile, yellow bile, phlegm, and blood—were thought to grow and subside within the body. These humors were directly related to the four elements: earth (black bile), fire (yellow bile), water (phlegm), and air (all four elements). An imbalance of these elements was thought to produce illness. Treatments such as bloodletting, emetics, and purges were procedures aimed at restoring balance to the body's humors.

Medical knowledge was the state directive of the Spanish, whose church–state consolidation of empire prohibited forays into experimental medicine. Miguel Serveto, the Spanish (Aragonese) physician and theologian, provides a telling example of what the Counter-Reformation climate was like for a medical innovator. He was the first European to describe respiratory circulation, but his research appeared in a theological treatise entitled *Christianismi restitutio,* in which he argued against predestination, saying that God did not condemn to hell people who had not committed evil in their lives. His rejection of both the Holy Trinity and predestination angered Catholics and Protestants alike. Most copies of the book were burned after it appeared in 1553, and a voice that opposed pro-Galenic orthodoxy by stating that blood passed through the lungs to the heart rather than through the septum was conflated with a voice that rejected religious orthodoxy. Serveto was burned at the stake outside Geneva in 1553 with one of his books chained to his leg.[14]

In such a climate, the Spanish naturalist Hernández held fast to the Hippocratic-Galenic perspective no matter where his gaze rested, and so a vast native pharmacology was rendered unintelligible before his eyes. His *Antigüedades de la Nueva España* demonstrates the doctor's disgust with native medical approaches, claiming that the nature and causes of illnesses were never analyzed, and that native medicines were prescribed with neither reason nor method.[15] As humoral theories were not to be found among the natives, Hernández imagined there was no system of medical explanation at all.

This hierarchy of cultural ideas about sickness contributed to the divide between the two care systems, and even though modern biomedical developments and new explanations have replaced classical theories, biomedicine continues to perform the same task undertaken by Hippocratic-Galenic thought during the first centuries of colonization: the naturalization of Western cultural superiority. William R. Holland's study of medicine in the mountainous regions of Chiapas conducted in the 1950s uncritically repeats the magic/science dichotomy that places Western thought at the summit of human cognitive potential. Working with INI, Holland is not unsympathetic to the extreme level of oppression to which the Tzeltal Mayans he studies were historically subjected. He reminds us that while Europeans and *ladinos* (ethnically Western people who reject indigenous heritage) used the sidewalk, Indians had to walk in the gutter, and until the time of the Mexican Revolution of 1910, Indians had to cross their arms and bow their heads when addressing a ladino. In certain areas, Indians were prohibited from riding horses well into the twentieth century. Holland acknowledges these social disparities as he carefully catalogues Tzeltal views of the universe and conceptions of pathology and wellness. However, when it comes to medical explanations, these are presented as a binary opposition between the sophistication of Western biomedicine and the puerile superstitions of Indians. Studies like Holland's are commonplace. An impassioned ethnographer acknowledges the disenfranchisement and oppression experienced by a group, writes enthusiastically about the pre-Hispanic traits that have survived despite years of colonial pressures, and then insists on the act of cataloguing practices and learning *about* "tribal ways," rather than entertaining the possibility of learning *from* non-Western knowledge systems.[16]

An example of this cultural paternalism is found when Holland shares his enthusiasm for the prospect of intercultural exchange in the medical sphere. Describing "complementary systems," Holland writes about a doctor from the Oxchuc clinic who was called to attend a Tzotzil man who had fallen, broken several ribs, and probably suffered from a collapsed lung. The gathered family members had little or no exposure to biomedical practices and had prepared themselves to accept the worst. Although INI discouraged the synthesis of traditional and Western practices, the doctor believed that circumstances called for an extraordinary intervention. He asked the patient's wife to bring him a hen. She produced the bird right away, and the doctor passed it over her husband in the form of a cross. He then decapitated the chicken, and when this was done, he passed a light over the patient's pupils to demonstrate to the family that the pupil did not respond to the stimulus. The doctor announced to the family that he had sacrificed the chicken and offered its spirit in exchange for the patient's. He illuminated the patient's pupil a second time, and everyone observed that his response had returned to normal. He then gave an injection of distilled water, explaining that it was highly effective in making sure that the soul remained in the body. The family was overjoyed by the treatment and its results and insisted that the doctor accept another chicken as a gesture of their gratitude.[17]

What Holland calls "complementary systems" are, in reality, the mimicry of Tzeltal ritual produced unreflectively. The doctor here does not collaborate with a separate cultural system. Somehow, the chicken and the injection achieved the desired results. This was not "complementary" care, but rather Western biomedicine condescending to play-act with its wards. Whereas the Inquisition had stopped short of being a hemispheric, totalizing force among the indigenous population because Indians were excluded from its jurisdiction, the colonial period's laissez-faire government transitioned into the biomedical era's outright contempt for the persistence of preconquest practices, and public power has steadily been aimed at replacing indigenous conceptions with biomedical ones.

It is necessary here to acknowledge the considerable contributions of Western medical practice. By standard measures, Mexico's rapid population growth (from 13.6 million in 1900 to 81.2 million in 1990) tells a success story of the health sector in the areas of immunization programs, child and prenatal care, sanitation, and nutrition. There is no case being made here for the abandonment of health institutions that provide biomedical training and care.[18] However, it is imperative to interrogate the cultural assumptions that accompany the introduction and proliferation of biomedical procedures, as these continue to encourage colonial orderings of epistemic authority. By imposing knowledge hierarchies based on elite access to medical competency, indigenous contributions to care may be extinguished before we have the opportunity to actualize what a culturally diverse pathway to wellness could be.

Strides toward intercultural dialogue are beginning to emerge. New organizations, primarily those formed between 1980 and the present, have begun to advocate conservation of Indian knowledge systems and the ecosystems on which these rely. The Centro de Desarrollo de la Medicina Maya was created in 1994 in San Cristobal de las Casas and is currently operated by Organización de Médicos Indígenas del Estado de Chiapas A.C. (OMIECH). The center runs a laboratory to develop medicines from indigenous plants, a museum of Tzotzil medicine, offices for administration, a teaching auditorium, and guest rooms for visitors. In 1995 IMSS–Solidaridad (Mexican Institute of Social Security–Solidarity) was created to foster relationships between indigenous and official care delivery programs in rural communities.[19]

In *El mandato de los dioses* (2005), Jaime Tomás Page Pliego points out that while public policy in Chiapas has moved toward the inclusion of indigenous curatives, the official agenda is the medicalization and professionalization of delivery in the region. Page Pliego writes that recent state legislation promising the inclusion of Mayan medicine proceeds

> como si los médicos indígenas y las comunidades estuvieran esperando la primera oportunidad para deshacerse de su medicina y recibir los parabienes, unos, de la atención biomédica, y otros, el conocimiento; dejándose, de lado, en primer término, que esos grupos participan de una visión de la realidad distinta de la que tiene la sociedad global, y, en segundo, la importancia histórica que para estos tiene la tradición médica, por integrar ideas y prácticas que de manera determinante han coadyuvado a su sobrevivencia física, cultural y espiritual, ante el constante embate de la sociedad colonial.[20]

> [as though the indigenous doctors and their communities had been waiting for the first opportunity to be rid of their own medicine and receive either the adulation of the biomedical establishment or its coveted information, abandoning, in the first place, any notion that these groups participate in a vision of reality that is entirely different from the one held by the global society, and in the second place, the historical significance that their medical traditions hold for them by integrating ideas and practices that have contributed vitally to their physical, cultural and spiritual survival under the relentless pummeling by colonial society.][21]

When true intercultural dialogue takes place, it will be characterized by indigenous agency and the respect for non-Western conceptual models. As Page Pliego points out, more than five hundred years after conquest, Mayan assimilation into the elite norm is still the national government's objective.

Curative Efficacy

When the Spanish doctor Nicolas Monardes wrote *Historia medicinal* in the late sixteenth century, his tone was that of unreserved appreciation of indigenous medical knowledge, claiming that the Spanish were to be reprehended for neglecting to pursue with real vigor and discipline the incredible richness of the native pharmacology. Unlike his contemporary Francisco Hernández, Monardes considered the Indians who sold their medicines in the marketplace to be great authorities on their wares and their myriad properties, having arrived at their conclusions through experimentation and discussion of their findings. He lamented that his countrymen gave no thought to the categorical dismissal of these native medical authorities who were custodians of an invaluable knowledge base and rebuked the shortsightedness of this colonial scorn.[22] This was no isolated voice of dissent; there were many like Monardes who did not contain their enthusiasm for native care. Hernán Cortés and his retinue were treated by Indian doctors after the battle of Otumba in 1520, and the viceroy Antonio de Mendoza was famously cured of what is thought to have been a serious meningeal or cerebral vascular illness by an Indian from Cuernavaca after having consulted all of the Spanish doctors living in New Spain at the time.[23]

The success of native care has been a well-documented, widespread aspect of the popular health sector. Informal knowledge was particularly tolerated in the area of obstetric care. In 1750, King Ferdinand VI had an exam structure created for midwives. In order to pass, purity of Spanish blood and three years of tutelage with an approved surgeon or midwife needed to be proven. By 1830 only two midwives had been approved: Angela Leite and Anastasia Recuerdo.[24] Obviously, these two midwives were not attending all of the births in the republic. This meant that all but two midwives were informally trained women, predominantly Indian or mestiza, who practiced in accordance with ancient ways.[25]

Hernández Sáenz and Foster argue that professionalization of the obstetric field, characterized by the increase of university-trained physicians specializing in this branch, led to the delegitimization of women practitioners. By reframing obstetrics as professional medicine, traditional *parteras* and even licensed midwives were reduced to secondary roles. Even so, their practices persisted and many preconquest practices continue to the present day.[26]

Sheila Cosminsky finds that with medicalization, pregnancy and childbirth are treated as abnormal states, to be regarded as emergencies. Under the professional biomedical system, the rural and traditional midwife must cede her way of knowing to the authority of university-trained obstetricians. Once the medical elite began to stake a claim in the territory of obstetrics and gynecology, this field that had previously been considered "denigrating" by male professionals would no longer be entrusted to the Indian and mestiza midwives who had for so long been its exclusive practitioners.[27]

Despite the tides of professionalization and medicalization that dehumanize or infantilize the intellectual resources of traditionally trained healers, indigenous doctors have been continually sought by local, national, and international patients, researchers, and students of non-Western medicine. Rosita Arvigo writes about her apprenticeship with a Mayan healer in *Sastun* (1995). An alternative health practitioner, Arvigo and her husband moved to Belize with their young child to live away from the toxicity of modern urbanism and to learn about traditional Mayan medicine. In the late 1980s, Michael J. Balick, director of the New York Botanical Garden Institute of Economic Botany, was appointed to search for medicinal plants with anticancer and anti-AIDS compounds in Central America. Arvigo's letter prompted him to take his search to Belize. Don Elijio Panti, a traditional doctor under whom Arvigo studied, chose twenty-five of his most important medicinal plants to be studied by the National Cancer Institute in Washington, D.C. Researchers usually find 1 to 5 percent of their collected specimens to show activity in their facilities. Don Elijio's collection showed a 25 percent rate of activity. Results from these tests were published in journals throughout the United States. This collaboration between Western ethnobotany, alternative health practice, and traditional curatives resulted in the foundation of the Ix Chel Tropical Research Foundation, forming a bridge between biomedicine and traditional curatives that then gave rise to other forms of coalitions. One such organization was the Belize Association of Traditional Healers (BATH). A priority of BATH is the promotion and furthering of traditional healing, but it is also designed to be a profit-sharing entity and provide some protection from the commercial exploitation of traditional healers and their knowledge. "We hope," writes Arvigo, "that this will encourage pharmaceutical companies to share their profits with the people from whose knowledge their drugs are derived."[28]

The emerging advocacy for indigenous healers' collectives has formidable opponents. The story of the multinational pharmaceutical industry, in its quest to develop new drugs, essential oils, and supplements, does not read unlike Juan Ponce de León's oft-narrated quest for the fountain of youth. The early conquistadors came to extract mineral wealth and spices and chart new trade routes. Today, researchers in pristine white lab coats frenetically scramble to stab indigenous minerals, flora, and fauna with the flag of their patron drug company. A famous example of this pioneering quest for profit is found in the ayahuasca (*Banisteriopsis caapi*) patent case.[29] Ayahuasca is a hallucinogenic plant held sacred by healers and priests of the Amazon. In 1986, Loren Miller, an American scientist and entrepreneur, obtained a US patent for a strain of the vine.[30] Although the patent was finally rejected in 1999, the "discovery" of the efficacy of native medicine by Western actors is a trope that is repeated again and again in international contact with indigenous health care in the Americas. In this glaring case of exploitation by the Western "entrepreneurial spirit," it is obvious that there is urgent need for native and international coalitions to promote the efficacy of their ecological and medical knowledge while securing protection from individuals and corporations that put profit before the survival of native peoples.

Representative Practices in the Americas Today

So far I have discussed the preponderance of native medicine in today's Mesoamerican regions and provided an overview of how the transmissions of indigenous healing managed to thrive despite the tides of early colonial and recent biomedical cultures. The present section looks at key roles that women fill in the health sector, to interpret the status of women and epistemic authority in contemporary Mesoamerica.

Generally speaking, neither women nor men who cure practice this occupation as the sole means of providing for themselves and their families. Economic survival in traditional Mesoamerican postconquest communities largely relies on agricultural labor, the sale of handcrafts, and, especially for women, household labor. For the most part, indigenous healers do not enjoy economic privilege, and they are frequently found among the poorest members of their villages. Therefore, social status and political authority are more important than remuneration in terms of the rewards this vocation can garner.

Parteras—Midwives

Carole Browner examines the social status of midwives in the Chinantec-speaking village of San Francisco in the highlands of Oaxaca and concludes that little elevation in status is associated with the specialization in midwifery in this community. Here the social pressures toward egalitarianism discourage women from differentiating themselves from their peers. In her fieldwork conducted between 1980 and 1981, it was revealed that 91 percent of the women respondents had delivered their last child at home without a nurse or physician present, and 82 percent used only herbal and other traditional remedies to recover from childbirth.

In San Francisco, individualistic advancement is discouraged in the public sector, and any claims to authority based on healing skills are criticized. Mothers are typically aware of the information distributed by midwives with regard to helpful herbs and strategies for a successful birth. In this type of social climate, the feature distinguishing Mesoamerican midwives from other women is not specialized knowledge of the physical demands of prenatal care, childbirth, or postpartum recovery, but rather the control of ritual knowledge, which is important to stave off illnesses caused by witchcraft. In the case of the San Francisco Chinantec region, midwives are valued and esteemed for their community involvements and selflessness instead of their competence as healers. As such, the role offers little advantage in terms of material benefits or political agency.[31]

Chinantec midwives are scarcely distinguishable from other women, and this is also the case among Lacandon Mayans of Chiapas. The Warraritari (Huichol) culture of northern Mexico puts such importance on the healing profession that the English translation of the Uto-Aztecan name of this nation is "doctors." In this group, healing is virtually an all-male domain. As with the Chinantec peoples, pregnancy and childbirth fall under the auspices of household medicine. If expectant or parturient mothers need assistance, a male priest-doctor will be called. Famous for their shamanism and prestige as healers, the Warraritari do not have a place for women in their hierarchy of sacred and medical ranks. Myerhoff (referred to in Dow 2001) mentions the existence of one female shaman but reports that she did not enjoy the same social status as her male counterparts.[32] Complex initiation and training rites govern access to curative works among the Warraritari, cementing a strictly male, strictly vertical conception of authority in the area of medical knowledge. Unlike the egalitarian situation of the Chinantec, in which healing expertise and midwifery are considered to belong to all members of the domestic sphere, a rigid hierarchy from which women are excluded characterizes the gendered world of Warraritari curing.[33]

Unlike the Chinantec and the Warraritari, the Mayans of the Pustunich community in the Yucatan Peninsula confer an elevated status to midwives, appreciable in the custom of employing the honorific "mah" before the midwife's name. In some places, a midwife may be asked to be a godmother to the child she delivers, or she is greeted with a bow and a kiss on her hand to show reverence. In many Mesoamerican groups, a degree of ambivalence accompanies such differentiation from the group. While their expertise and commitment may be respected, midwives will also report that they are criticized for behaving contrary to prescribed gender norms: they travel alone, have influence outside the domestic sphere, stand to make their own money (although this is invariably a small sum), and are prone to being struck by arrows of fear and envy because of their spiritual powers.[34]

Cosminsky situates the status of Mayan midwifery in the context of biomedical pressures to obtain official training and licensing through the Ministry of Health. In a postconquest environment in which both ladino and indigenous conceptions of health care are present, the traditional midwife ranks lowest in terms of epistemic authority. Cosminsky describes the government midwifery programs designed to train "traditional birth attendants" (TBAs) as "ethnocentric" and "medicocentric," as they apply a biomedical definition to the role of the midwife, who, in the Mesoamerican context, is much more than the person who attends a birth. In many cases, parteras provide prenatal and postnatal care, as well as the socio-spiritual equilibrium that defines indigenous conceptions of wellness.[35]

Curanderas—Healers

It was not until the arrival of Spaniards that the general term *curandero* arose. Rather, notes Viesca, "the curandero is the product of the conquest: indigenous medical specialists such as the Nahua ticitl, the

Huastec ilalix, the Tzeltal h'ilojel and Tzotzil h'ilol, the Mayan h-men, the ah cut of the Pokoman, and its Quiché equivalent, the ah cun, became diluted and homogenized."[36] These different terms indicate the cultural and ecological diversity of Mesoamerica, uniquely coded comprehensions of bodily structure and function, distinct concepts of the origin of illness and its role in the integrity of the community, and vastly different vocabularies for distinguishing medical and spiritual specialists from other community actors. Without a full inquiry into a group's conception of the physiological being, the implications of these different designations remain obscure. Nevertheless, it is important here to attempt an overview of what *curanderismo* encompasses, since this is the term most often used to refer to "popular" or "folk" healers today.

Women practitioners are represented in all the healing specializations, which constitute a continuum ranging between physical and spiritual ailments and remedies, and those that sit somewhere in between. Among "secular" specialists are the *hueseros* (bone setters), *sobadores* (massage therapists), and *yerberos* (herbalists). Naturalistic knowledge of medicinal plants and techniques defines the latter group, but among Mesoamerican healers of all stripes a spiritual relationship to native flora and fauna is pervasive.

In Holland's study of Tzotzil medicine, he discusses three categories of healers. The *ts'ak bak* has the lowest status, employing a combination of spiritual and natural remedies, with an area of specialization limited to the less urgent matters. Usually this type of healer begins to cure when a family member is in need. Knowledge of cures comes from the ancestral mountain deities, who teach their chosen students how to set broken bones and alleviate pain. The successful outcome of a treatment becomes known to others, who then solicit cures. The ts'ak bak would be the closest to the broadly defined "curandera." Rashes, broken bones, infection, and other complaints that would be handled by a general practitioner or osteologist in the West are treated by the ts'ak bak in the Tzotzil highlands, where there is no such thing as a purely laic area of health care. The ts'ak bak cures the physical ailments, but does this by engaging both the physical and the spiritual planes. Prayers are offered, but rituals and sacred petitions are less elaborate than those offered by the *'ilol* and *me'santo,* both of which are categorized more accurately in Western discussions under the designation of shaman.[37]

In the Purépecha community of Pichátaro, curanderas are almost exclusively women, the majority of whom come from families in which mothers and grandmothers were also healers. The art of curing is not a full-time, well-paid occupation. Curanderas use herbal remedies, most of which are harvested on the lands around Pichátaro. Instead of being isolated from Western influence, the Pichátaro community represents a mix of Spanish and Purépecha cultures. Among Mexico's indigenous populations, their town enjoys a higher standard of living than most, which means that a solid majority can rely on piped water sources and electricity. As with other Indian communities, agriculture is the central occupation, and the household is the most important social group. As a matrilineal transmission of knowledge, the practice of curanderismo amongst Purépechan women deals mostly with gastrointestinal disorders and emotion-based illnesses, while illnesses resulting from witchcraft are taken to "good witches" or shamans.[38]

Chamanas—*Shamans*

Shaman originally referred to native Turkic-Mongol healers of Siberia and Mongolia, meaning "he or she who knows." Mircea Eliade defines the shaman as a healer who relies on the ecstatic journey—an altered state of consciousness—to interact with the divine in order to cure. Involuntary or self-induced trances, meditative rhapsodies, prophetic visions and dreams, and the mediation of these states on behalf of their patients are all attributes of the shaman's calling. In the Americas, shamans that provided messages from the gods were the earliest representatives of religious, political, and medical authority. Here the word is reluctantly employed, with the understanding that Mesoamerican communities in which shamans figure prominently, as with curanderos, have their own designations for the office. The role of the chamana differs from that of curanderas and parteras in that the chamana occupies a position of authority in the community. A hierarchy is present in which the chamana fulfills a priestess avocation, rather than serving in the more laic branches of curanderismo and midwifery.

Among the Tzotziles in Chiapas, for example, a clear hierarchy of care providers is discernable among practitioners. Above the general curanderismo practiced by the ts' ak bak, we find the complex repertoire of spiritual rituals offered by the 'ilol. Because more elaborate methods involving the spiritual plane are incorporated at this level of delivery, the 'ilol fits the "shaman" designation. In Holland's study, women will fill the role of 'ilol but do not advance to the next rung of me'santo, which is an office combining civic and religious responsibilities along with the mastery of the highest level of spiritual mysteries. Many scholars of Mesoamerican gender roles and ideology note that the political-religious-medical areas are frequently conflated under the auspices of the shamanic vocation, and in the majority of cases in which gender behavior prohibits women from sharing in public political activity, their shamanic practice will also be limited in scope to the healing aspect of their shamanic functions. In such environments, men tend to occupy the political and priestly roles associated with an exceptional control of the spirit entities that permit successful healing and counter the workings of evil spells.

Tzotzil 'ilols treat all manner of internal and external conditions that tend to be caused by supernatural agents. The ceremonies of the 'ilols distinguish them from the curanderismo of the ts'ak bak, whose repertoire of curatives is limited to the laic, empirical paradigm. In contrast, the successful 'ilol is indeed a powerful person. Because illness is conceived as divine punishment, or in many cases, as the misconduct of sorcerers, the supernatural advocacy of the 'ilol is an extraordinary path. The status of an 'ilol is inferior only to that of the me'santo in the hierarchy governing Tzotzil wisdom and social leadership. According to Holland, the me'santo office excludes women, yet he also discusses a husband-and-wife team in which a me'santo is married to an 'ilol, and they practice healing together.

Among the Chatino in the southeast of Oaxaca, half of the respondents who identified themselves as healers in an INI study were women. One-third of the group practiced the kind of healing that incorporates the ecstatic journey and a direct communion with the divine to diagnose illness and prognosticate its course. Among the Chatino, there are no mentors or guides. Most frequently, an individual experiencing an incurable illness ingests psychotropic mushrooms and is instructed by spirit beings as to how the illness should be treated. Once they recover, they go on to heal other members of the family, and word about their successful cures spreads throughout the community.

The ailments caused by espanto (*atzoi cua*) and witchcraft are fought by shamans. *Brujería* in particular requires the intervention of a skilled shaman, who will often diagnose the cause and prescribe a plan of treatment based on the altered states of consciousness produced by psychoactive substances. As these common illnesses require powerful spiritual mediation, women with shamanic potencies are imbued with significant spiritual and civic agency.

In Mazatec shamanism of the highlands of Oaxaca, where over half the healers are reported to be women, female practitioners have famously accessed the highest echelons of epistemic authority. María Sabina, whose life and works are explored more fully in the next chapter, is known throughout the world for her calling as a Mazatec healer-priestess, officiant of the mushroom ritual, and author of medicine chants. While the need to individuate healers and thinkers has been imposed on her unusual abilities by international actors, her increased fame did little to earn her wealth or status within her own community. In her biography by Álvaro Estrada, the author is dismayed by the solitude and squalor surrounding her at the end of her days. The indigenous conception of success as a centrifugal force is directly at odds with Western notions of transcendence. Individuation, ambition, and personal gain potentially remove shamans from the matrix of meaning on which their ability to cure is contingent.

Conclusion

When Western colonization subjugated the Mesoamerican civilizing project in the New World, indigenous women healers were removed from the sphere of intellectual legitimacy. In the early days of the colony and republic, they were unable to enter into the official training programs and university courses that would grant them epistemic authority in the eyes of the state; when biomedicine replaced classical medical explanations, their knowledge traditions were regarded as a symptom of Latin American backwardness. Either caught under the scrutiny of biomedical criteria, where traditional practitioners are classified as retrograde and superstitious, or circumvented by profit-seeking multinational pharmaceutical companies, the survival of traditional practices, once tolerated as a tactic for the preservation of Spanish hegemony, has come under threat by the tides of globalization.

Millennial Western doublespeak is evident in the popular *Survivorman* series: a television star equipped with detailed knowledge about how to benefit from the local ecology calmly tells his tale of rugged privations to the camera audience at home. Though the tested hero makes a meal of grasshoppers or grubs, he will soon be flown home to his own comfortable neighborhood, schedule a serious talk with his agent about his book deal, and have his high-end survival attire laundered by domestic workers.

Mesoamerican women who have guarded the transmission of their knowledge from the apocalypse wrought by Western invasion are not portrayed as clever, rugged, and amicable dwellers of the American frontier. The true survivors are those who were shooed to the outside of the camera frame, and who taught Survivorman how not to die on the first day of filming. In a week's time he gleefully leaves the place of the Inuit and the Waorani and flies back to civilization without a backward glance at the people who make an unremarked survival episode out of each day of their lives. Because women healers have been engaged in centrifugal forms of knowledge production and transmission, their individual identities are largely subsumed by a cultural context that awards communal notions of identity and transcendence. Mesoamerican women thinkers do not step onto center stage as patent-owning pharmaceutical entrepreneurs, doctors, inventors, philosophers, or reality show stars. Their works have endured the centuries-old legacy of colonization in large part owing to a cultural preference for social and ecological balance. Centripetal conceptions of intellectual agency would be widely regarded in Mesoamerican cultures as a kind of pathology—an egoism that is ultimately destructive and more akin to the category of witchcraft than to that of wisdom. By consuming Mesoamerican and indigenous knowledge and the ecological and cultural environments in which this knowledge is produced, the Western hunger is a greater threat to indigenous survival than any that has come before, as it defines science, reason, and progress as the sedimentation of Western man's supremacy.

5

AluciNet.ion

Spiritual Capital in the Sierra Mazateca

HUAUTLA DE JIMÉNEZ, 1998. My friends Dominica, Xochitl, and I are in a small shack that rests upon a packed-dirt floor over which small insects casually migrate. Beams of light slip through the many spaces between the wooden slats. My son Emiliano is outside with Dominica's partner, Carlos, who did not want to participate in the ceremony. It was against Carlos's principles to exchange money for "spiritual services." As we await the return of Agustina Martinez, the shaman who will bring us the honguitos (mushrooms) and officiate the ceremony, Dominica describes Carlos's relationship to the Lakota sweat lodge practice and his Native American friends who caution him against buying products or experiences from purveyors of native "wisdom." I remember the Lakota sweat lodge that I had visited with Dominica and Carlos, and the way our host had advised us against the purchase of copal incense or sweetgrass because it was impossible to know the energy or intent of the person who harvested them.

Yet here I am in Mexico, the highlands of Oaxaca, where the children of doña Agustina's family go without shoes in the summertime. They have no plumbing, and when it becomes necessary for us to use the toilet, they explain that a storm has knocked over their outhouse and that we should simply find a place "over there"—referring to the bushes and hillside surrounding us. My mind does not know how to integrate the disparate strands of information regarding the commodification of the mushroom ceremony. I cannot say with total honesty that I trust the person that I am paying. But I can sincerely say that I mistrust my own suspicions, and the media streams of information upon which they are based.

Huautla de Jiménez, 2002. At the time of completing my dissertation on women and knowledge in Mesoamerica at Columbia University, I took a trip to Huautla with my friends Amado and Daniel. We noticed a mural emblazoned on the wall of one of the two Internet cafés that were thriving that season. The café was called "AluciNet.*ion*." A picture of the honguito serving as satellite dish proudly portrays the far reach of local customs. The multiple fonts in the lettering allow a playful range of readings: hallucination/hallucin-nation/hallucin-Net-tion/and so on. The mushroom is the grounded, symbolic center of the image, responsible for its own broadcast waves, choosing its own direction that leans toward the café's name, in which ecstasy, nation, and technology merge while their separateness remains intact.

Ten years after the first visit, much has changed: my relationship to Huautla, my bond with doña Agustina, my son's need for supervision, my research. My project then had been to find a portal into my own identity, to do what Chicana theorist Norma Alarcón has called the recovery of "lost origins": "a profound spiritual kinship with the 'lost'—a spirituality whose resistant political implications must not be underestimated, but refocused for feminist change."[1] Certainly Mesoamerican and North American spiritualities provide strategies for the decolonial projects of Chicanos and Chicanas, but with the benefit of hindsight, I appreciate how my early misgivings about the situation in 1998 evoked the more essentialist shadings of the pursuit of "the" Indian experience and lacked the focus on feminist change in their veneration of a past "utopia." This essentialism is described by Frantz Fanon in *The Wretched of the Earth* (1963) as the "second stage" in the development of revolutionary consciousness.

According to Fanon, the first phase in the development of a decolonial mentality consists of "unqualified assimilation," in which the colonizer's language and aesthetics are used to contest the colonizer's views point by point. This mimicry of forms and concepts constitutes a pure reaction to colonial hegemony, devoid of sympathy for the precolonial imagination. The second phase is one in which the native rediscovers his or her own people, and former arts and poetics are reinterpreted, albeit through the mediation of colonial mentality. This phase is typified by the mining of particularisms, the trotting-out of indigenous achievements in a voyeuristic or two-dimensional manner that finds the native cultural innovator acting as a foreigner. The second phase offers a postcard, sound-bite vision of the world that existed before the colony, and it tends to reduce a culture's significance to the nostalgia for local customs. The third phase is characterized by the emergence of the voices of the colonized, as testimonial works decry the abuses of the colonizer. The revolutionary phase finally rejects both the colonizer's poetics and an essentialist stock of particularisms, in order to promote an aesthetic of political struggle. Fanon writes, "In an underdeveloped country during the period of struggle traditions are fundamentally unstable and are shot through by centrifugal tendencies."[2] As with Fanon's work, my process has been one of recuperating that which has been effaced by the colonial imagination, while at the same time locating solutions that correspond to the mutable nature of identity and culture. This outward force that flees the center, where political power and elite discourse collude in the ossification of colonial norms, compares to the transmission of healing in Mesoamerican cultures, where equilibrium and collectivity are the markers of wellness, and the reification of ego and hierarchies are symptoms of pathology.

To probe the implications of the "fugue" paradigm a bit further, Western clinical psychiatry offers us the intriguing diagnosis of the "fugue state" or "dissociative fugue," when people seem confused about their identity. This complex type of seizure is usually characterized by reversible amnesia for personal characteristics, such as memories, personal identity, and personality. This rare condition of altered consciousness often involves unplanned travel or wandering and the replacement of the former identity with an entirely different one. To those who experience the consequences of colonization, puzzlement over the individual identity and serious memory disorder do not threaten the stability of normative personality, but rather constitute the only personality development trajectory available.

The cultural innovator who strives to see a new social structure emerge will neither lament the instability brought about by fugue nor long nostalgically for a "lost utopia":

> It is not enough to try to get back to the people in that past out of which they have already emerged; rather we must join them in that fluctuating movement which they are just giving shape to, and which, as soon as it has started, will be the signal for everything to be called in question. Let there be no mistake about it; it is to this zone of occult instability where the people dwell that we must come; and it is there that our souls are crystallized and that our perceptions and our lives are transfused with light.[3]

Fanon's stages in the evolution of a decolonial cultural production maintain that resistance to colonization must not amount to fixed forms of behavior that disallow culture's permeable nature. While I do not propose that emancipatory cultural production always presents itself in these discrete, sequential movements, Fanon's scheme is useful in developing an understanding of the aims and pitfalls of decolonial cultural practice. In retrospect, it certainly seems that I sought a bona fide shaman to unlock the meaning of "the" lost, indigenous past. Fanon concludes that the second stage is tantamount to self-stereotyping, because it peers at one's own culture through the colonizer's gaze and reduces it into a catalogue of fetishes and curios. This chapter tells the story of real-life shaman women, and how they managed to frustrate my quest for the iconic. By pursuing a name, face, or symbol that would serve as the Rome or Mecca of my pilgrimage, I was insisting on a binary construction of Anahuac, a magical realm that existed within a vacuum where the shamanic journey, such as the one present in Fanon's stages described above, is never tempered to increase its durability, balance, and strength.

In the previous chapters I have attempted to situate the knowledge production of Mesoamerican women within different historical circumstances. Here, I will explore the ways in which contemporary native Mazatec traditions interact with First World markets. To do this, I discuss the position of women shamans in light of the Western categories of "knowledge" and "authenticity." Drawing on globalization scholarship and performance studies, I interpret the Mazatec mushroom ritual, and the shaman women that officiate this ritual, as indigenous resistance to colonial oppression.

In the case of the shamans in Huautla de Jiménez, we are presented with a paradox. On one hand, the local chamana represents cultural resistance in the face of the intrusion of Mexica, Spanish, and Occidental imperialist forces. On the other hand, her work with foreigners can lead us to the most dystopian images of a new world order, in which the demise of traditional medicine is blamed on her propagation of sacred ways. Now, Huautla de Jiménez is a site for spiritual tourism, a place that national and international travelers visit to buy mushrooms to ingest on their own, to sell, or to eat in the context of the ceremony. The transformation of the ceremony into a commodity has provided a source of income and vitality for the families that supply mushrooms to outsiders and for the associated industries. Women sell white cotton blouses embroidered with the mushroom; young men act as tour guides; the town's three hotels are packed during the rainy season, when the honguito thrives; restaurants, bars, and markets profit more than during other times of the year. To understand whether a productive interdependence between Mesoamerican and Western civilizing projects can take place, I needed to explore the discourses and performances that frame shamanism during a global age. Álvaro Estrada's biography entitled *María Sabina: Her Life and Chants* has been particularly useful in understanding the early introduction of the Mazatec mushroom ritual to foreigners. Estrada, a Mazatec scholar, created this volume between the years of 1975 and 1976 from a series of interviews with María Sabina. With translation and commentary prepared by Henry Munn, this text also provides a critical introduction to the ceremony for those unfamiliar with Mazatec customs or mycology. Also, the friendship and hospitality of Agustina Martinez, the woman I mistrusted on the occasion of my first mushroom ceremony in 1998, have challenged me to consider the relationship between local and global flows in less vertical terms.

Altered States

María Sabina, the Mazatec shaman woman who introduced the mushroom ceremony to the hippie generation and brought international attention to Huautla de Jiménez, relates the story of her collaboration with the Harvard anthropologist Gordon Wasson, claiming that the mushrooms, traditionally ingested during healing ceremonies that she officiated for members of her community, no longer spoke her language after their consumption by outsiders. She practiced her shaman's vocation during the first wave of non-Mazatec consumers and insisted that no wise person should ever prosper from the commerce of mushrooms. Agustina Martinez, a healer who is currently practicing in the highlands of Oaxaca, exchanges the ceremony and the mushroom for a fee to tourists and adventurers. Sharing her practice with spiritual tourists some forty years after the hippie generation, Martinez attends to local, traditional maladies but also runs a rustic pension (no plumbing, cement floors, wood-plank beds) for the tourists, plainly exercising the dual callings of both wise woman and businesswoman.

Doña María and doña Agustina have permitted new ways for foreigners to participate in the intimacy of Mazatec spiritual practices. Before outsiders had crossed Sabina's threshold, the ceremony had specific, exclusive applications within the Mazatec world. The wise ones did not go about propagating what they did. The shamanic world and the ceremony itself were highly delicate, private matters, not even to be discussed among wise people. Her local fame resulted from the word-of-mouth publicity of grateful clients that she had successfully cured, and the ceremony was never conducted for people who were not sick. With the arrival of international visitors, Sabina found herself consenting to perform ceremonies for the multitudes of outsiders that came to her not because they suffered from symptoms of illness, but because they wanted to "see God." These were not locals coming to her to perform ceremonies to alleviate toothache, pregnancy discomfort, and the maladies attributable to sorcery or the various enchantments of the soul to which she was accustomed, but a very different kind of clientele.

Today, the sacred mushroom is emblazoned on souvenir shirts and appears as an emblem on the towels of Huautla's Primero de Mayo motel. The sons of Martinez and other locals often greet arriving buses to see if they can be of assistance to visitors, offering to arrange for a ceremony. These outsiders are not in apparent need of medical attention, but Martinez and Sabina before her made the sacred mushroom available to all.

The new world order, a phrase I am using to describe the dominance of neoliberal economic and political models in the Americas as well as globalized flows of culture, capital, and people, has a specific impact on Indian women of Mexico, which must be investigated in the context of the history of Mexican colonial notions of female indigeneity. With its roots in the troubling case of La Malinche, history reveals that men along with women were the hosts of often-fickle loyalties during the throes of the Spanish conquest of indigenous Mesoamerica. Malinche is often credited with (or accused of) having borne the first mestizos, and arguably her distinction as the mother of Mexican miscegenation, however divorced from the early accounts of Cortés and his retinue, remains fixed, whether as a stubborn spiritual truth, or a foundational myth, or a folktale.

The color and seduction of the Malinche myth allow it to usurp historical evidence of male collaboration in the victory of the Spanish conquest, as it corresponds more readily than history to what Octavio Paz elaborates in *The Labyrinth of Solitude* as being the "true" nature of the Mexican people: a submerged inferiority complex that stems from Malinche's betrayal. While it is well known that the Tarascan Empire was allied with Cortés and made it possible for his small retinue to defeat the Mexica, it is Malinche's role that has helped her name become synonymous with national treason. This foundational archetype of Mexico's early connection with international forces divulges the ready-made script of female treachery. Contemporary feminists have revised this myth, decrying the patriarchal context in which women were enslaved and objectified. As Gloria Anzaldúa has poignantly put it, "not me sold out my people but they me."[4] Feminists point out that Malinche had been a slave, sold first by her own mother to please her new husband, and then given to Cortés as battle spoils. She was not a citizen who could betray, but rather a slave within the imperial Mexica regime whose patriarchal social order had excluded her from the state.

From the historical insistence on Malinche as a Mexican Eve, culpable for her people's eviction from paradise, current attitudes about contact with outside forces continue to disproportionately level charges against women. In terms of the negotiation of spiritual capital, women who assimilate outside market patterns do so in the shadow of La Malinche. Jane Hill, in "Women's Speech in Modern Mexicano," sheds light on the gender dynamics in modern Nahuatl-speaking communities. Among Nahuatl-speaking women living in (and this is coincidental) the Malinche Volcano communities in the central Mexican states of Puebla and Tlaxcala, the women demonstrated less blending of the Nahuatl and Spanish languages than did the men. Her findings reveal that "women are more conservative than men in cases of stable variation, but are more innovative in cases of change in progress, particularly if the change is an assimilation toward the elite norm."[5] This means that the women, less exposed to the workforce, factories, and the social milieu in which men reside, are found to retain more Nahuatl, but when they speak Spanish, their Spanish is less influenced by Nahuatl than that of the men.

Because women are "more conservative" than men, they tend to be monolingual Nahuatl speakers in greater numbers than their male counterparts. Thus, it is the women who bear the stigma of lagging behind the times, as colonial shame is attached to the condition of monolingualism. The opposite stigma is attached to speaking only Spanish, violating the pact of solidarity within this Nahuatl-speaking group. The women seem to bear the brunt of the negative implications of either of these scenarios. Hill comments:

> In the matter of Mexicano [Nahuatl], however, nothing of what women do is valued by men. . . . Thus the failure of women to conform to male norms may be a result of exclusion from them rather than of some special affinity of women to elite norms. . . . Women may find that the symbolic resources emanating from an urban elite are a good alternative to male usage patterns, offering benefits that may be more attractive to women, who are excluded from scarce resources in their own community. . . .[6]

Women's speech patterns in modern Nahuatl make it clear that they are ready to reject masculine ways of communicating in favor of foreign ones, not because of a desire to reproduce elite language patterns, but because these are more tenable to women than male language patterns from within their own community. When women are undervalued by the men in their group, the historical Malinche's lot comes to mind: when a woman is viewed as object rather than as actor by her local community, foreign solutions become a logical route toward the self-preservation and determination to which all humans aspire.

The market choices faced by shaman women of the Sierra Mazateca reflect a situation that is not unlike that of the Malinche Volcano community. Because they realize greater possibilities for economic determination from external flows than from local or national ones, many will readily adapt foreign values into their practices. In my capacity as participant observer in the Sierra Mazateca, I have seen and experienced a complete division between men and women that places men at the center of social gatherings and women on the periphery as their attendants. On one occasion, as the comadre (godmother) of two of Agustina Martinez's grandchildren, I hosted a party for my godchildren, for which I paid for ten cases of beer, the consumption of which became the exclusive right and privilege of the men of the family and their invited male guests. At the party I sponsored, I naively sat down to enjoy a Corona with my Mazatec *compadre* (fellow godparent) when he offered it to me, but soon doña Agustina gestured for me to come away from the male arena, and I realized that throughout the afternoon and into the night, no woman but I had ventured near the table around which the men sat drinking and playing CDs of traditional ballads celebrating horses and Pancho Villa. This was particularly perplexing to me as it had been I, a woman, who had treated the group to all the rounds. Also, my own family is populated by some energetic drinkers, and the ritual of tying one on is not the exclusive territory of males or maleness in my social universe. However, in Huautla the women served the men food when they were asked to and picked up the glass from various bottles that had slipped from the grasp of people who were so inebriated that maintaining a firm hold on their bottle had become difficult. I either remained in the kitchen, where the women gathered near a wood-burning stove and chatted in Mazatec, or sat outside on a bench that was arranged alongside the male circle, where I nursed an orange soda and watched my friend Amado consume what he described as "more beer than I've drunk since high school" with the men.

This gendered prohibition extends to other areas of the Martinez family life as well. My understanding is that the men of the family are ceremonially introduced to the mushroom ritual when they are about thirteen years old and considered to have come of age. The women receive no such induction. The youngest Martinez daughter was about twenty years old during my visit in 2002 and had never eaten the mushrooms, because it was considered more important for the family's survival to offer them to visitors who could afford to give something in return. I offered to pay for her ceremony on one occasion, but she had other commitments that prevented her from accepting my offer.

Unlike María Sabina, Agustina Martinez has been married only once and, by all appearances, enjoys a strong union with her husband. Sabina had loved Serapio Martinez, her first husband, who routinely brought other women into their home for periods that ranged from two weeks to a month. She bore Serapio three children, but when he died of pneumonia he bequeathed his animals and money to a girlfriend that lived in the Mazatec lowlands. Marcial Carrera, Sabina's second husband, was an indolent drunk who womanized and beat her. The children of one of the women with whom he was involved wounded him with a machete, and he bled to death in the street. After her second marriage ended with Carrera's death, and no longer governed by the cruelty of these marriages, Sabina was able to dedicate herself to her calling and preserve the sanctity of the mushroom ritual that demands sexual abstinence.

For the women of the Sierra Mazateca, songs celebrating horsemanship and the glories of bravely fought battles of the revolution by men do little to alter their felt conditions of servitude and the devaluation of their labor as mothers, cooks, seamstresses, farmers, and tradeswomen. Marriage, the locally and nationally sanctioned contract that permits women to share the households of men who enjoy greater social and economic privilege than they do, does not guarantee an improvement of women's social or economic conditions. In her study of economic globalization, Saskia Sassen presents a view of emancipation that compares to that of Anzaldúa and like critics who claim that a transnational context alters gender patterns, and that the emergence of transnational households can empower women.[7] In other words, if assimilation to the male norm that defines national inclusion is impossible in a misogynistic setting, then looking outside the nation can be a step forward in the pursuit of women's emancipation.

For a Mazatec group that struggles to maintain ethnic coherence in the face of a centralist Mexican government, the mushroom ritual constitutes an act of resistance and had functioned as such even before the arrival of the Spanish. When the Mexica invaded the northern highlands of Oaxaca, the Mazatecs allied themselves with the Tlaxcalans and Mixtecs in various battles against these foes that were considered to be vicious flesh-eaters.[8] The Spaniards came next, but as precious metals were not forthcoming in the region, agricultural tribute was demanded instead. In the face of Mexica, Spanish, and transnational, neocolonial invasion, the *shuta tshinea* (wise women and men) conserve rituals that express political, social, and religious beliefs central to the integrity of their community.

The performative nature of the chamana's activity constitutes what James C. Scott calls a "hidden transcript" of resistance. The notion of the inversion of the powerful and the weak can be found in "every major cultural tradition in which inequities of power, wealth, and status have been pronounced. . . . These collective hidden transcripts from the fantasy life . . . are embedded . . . in innumerable ritual practices . . . and have provided the ideological basis for many revolts."[9] This is not to present the ritual practice of Mexico's traditional healers as a springboard for insurgence, but rather to acknowledge that its endurance through the tides of conquest and colonization represents a site in which preconquest form has managed to articulate the Mesoamerican identity in spite of the dominant culture that privileges Western conceptions of truth.

The ritual is certainly far removed from Western clinical care delivery. The *velada* is held at night and indoors.[10] The mushrooms, *psilocibina mexicana* Heim, are called *di shi toó* (little things that spring forth) or *di shi santo* (saint children) in the Mazatec language. Images of Christ, the Virgin, and saints are often present in the ceremony, but I am told that these are not universal. For the Catholic Mazatec, the ingestion of the mushroom is syncretic with the flesh of Christ. All who participate, shaman and patient, must abstain from sexual relations, but the amount of time for which they observe this fast varies. Agustina Martinez asks all of her visitors who participate in the ceremony to abstain on the day of the ceremony and for four days afterward. Copal incense is used for purification, and fresh candles are lit. The officiant sings or prays for his or her patient.

I include a segment of one of María Sabina's chants here to elucidate the particulars of shamanic language, which was a central aspect of the cure.

> Tú santo, tú Cristo
> Tú eres el Santo Niño de Atocha
> Tú San Isidro

Padre labrador, padre rico
Padre fresco, padre tierno
Santo, santa, santo
Todavía hay santos, todavía hay santas
Tú eres mujer luna
Mujer estrella grande, mujer estrella cruz
Mujer estrella Dios
[y repite]
Tú eres Luna
Tú eres mujer estrella grande
Mujer estrella Dios
Mujer estrella cruz
Madre Guadalupe, madre Concesa
Madre patrona, madre Natividad
Madre Concepción
. . .
Soy mujer águila dueña, dice
Soy mujer tlacuache dueña, dice
Soy mujer que examina, dice
Es Jesucristo, dice
Soy mujer limpia, dice
Mujer que truena, dice
Mujer que es arrancada, dice
Soy mujer Ustandí debajo de agua, dice
Soy mujer Ustandí debajo de lo sagrado, dice
Soy mujer aerolito, dice
. . .
—¿No es así? [María Sabina]
—Sí, es así . . . [Cayetano]
[Un breve silencio, después María Sabina termina diciendo:]
¿Qué dificultad hay para hacer esto?[11]

You, saint; you, Christ
You are the Saint Child of Atocha
You, San Isidro
Worker father, rich father
Fresh father, tender father
Saint, saintess, saint

Yet there are saints, yet there are saintesses
You are moon woman
Great star woman, cross star woman
God star woman
[this repeats]
You are Moon
You are big star woman
Star God woman
Star cross woman
Mother Guadalupe, Mother Concesa
Mother Superior, Mother Nativity
Mother Conception
. . .
I am eagle chief woman, it says
I am marmot chief woman, it says
I am woman that examines, it says
It is Jesus Christ, it says
I am clean woman, it says
Woman that thunders, it says
I am woman Ustandi under the water, it says
I am woman Ustandi beneath the sacred, it says
I am woman meteorite, it says
. . .
Is it not so?
Yes, it is so . . . (Cayetano)
[A brief silence, after which María Sabina finishes by saying:]
What difficulty is there in this?

Most of these mushroom medicine songs obey similar formal principles. They chant in short enunciations in first-person singular, ending with the word *tso,* which translates into English as "it says," and into Spanish as "dice." Functioning as the mouthpiece for the volition of the mushroom, this repeated "it says" conveys what the *niños* tell the shaman's clients. Henry Munn explains that the first-person-singular verb form that predominates in velada chanting is not used to indicate that the shaman herself becomes a "star cross" or "Jesus Christ." Rather, this ceremony serves as a powerful curative because it leads participants on a journey in which the egocentric "I" is replaced by the abstract and the universal. Munn writes: "María Sabina becomes what she names and at the same time her listeners are led by her words to feel their own egos extended beyond themselves to become all things."[12] A key aspect of the mushroom's curative efficacy is how it helps the patient to surrender ego and selfhood. As has been discussed in previous chapters, the Mesoamerican health sector combats the excesses of ego in its many forms. Mushroom poetry cures with this transcendence.

To accommodate non-Mazatec consumers, the mushroom ceremony has undergone various adaptations. While María Sabina sang or chanted under the effect of the mushroom, Agustina Martinez does not consume the mushroom in the ceremony that she officiates for tourists, and the songs are often from the Catholic Church, along with prayers and supplications that she makes in Mazatec. Also, before the foreigners came along, Sabina had used the velada only for medicinal purposes—never as recreation. In his preface to the English-language edition, Wasson laments his own role in the occidentalization of Huautla.[13] After he experienced the ceremony, María Sabina claimed that the mushrooms did not work anymore, and that there was nothing that anyone could do to restore them: "But from the moment the foreigners arrived to search for God, the saint children lost their purity. They lost their force; the foreigners spoiled them. From now on they won't be any good. There's no remedy for it."[14]

Sabina's claim that the mushroom language had been lost and the virtue of its healing properties spoiled is remarked by Wasson, who, in his essay appearing at the beginning of Henry Munn's English edition of Sabina's testimony, writes, "These words make me wince: I, Gordon Wasson, am held responsible for the end of a religious practice in Mesoamerica that goes back far, for millennia. I fear she spoke the truth, exemplifying her wisdom."[15] Reading Wasson's lament, I do not think that Sabina's words allow for such a literal interpretation, or such a naive conception of one person's influence. We can begin to problematize Sabina's dark prognostication first by understanding some of the implications of the word *language* within the tradition of Mazatec wise ones. A difficulty of translating Sabina's chants is that her words come from the mushrooms themselves, and not from the lexicon of everyday Mazatec usage. One of Munn's learned Mazatec consultants, when pressed to transcribe Sabina's poetry, exclaimed,

"Who knows where the old lady gets her words from!" Estrada explained that Sabina enjoyed the obscurity of her phrases, refusing to define words for translators, offering the simple explanation that they were "mushroom language."[16] Her hidden poetry resisted Western facsimile when she was alive, and the testimony of her life as a wise one equally resists literal translation now that she is gone.

The language wise people use is a blending of riddle, prescription, and augury and is *not* intended to function in the same way as ordinary exchange. The fact that wise ones are not in dialogue with each other about their cures tells us that this form of healing resists the confines of linear utterance, particularly for its master practitioners. To this point, Friedrich Nietzsche provides a remark that might have been written for Wasson. "Every profound spirit needs a mask; nay, more, around every profound spirit there continually grows a mask, owing to the constantly false, that is to say *superficial* interpretation of every word he utters, every step he takes, every sign of life he manifests."[17] With his superficial interpretation of Sabina's claim, Wasson passes up the chance to explore her words as a statement with depth and breadth about cultures in contact, and chooses to make it about his own circumstances.

Wasson is aggrieved when he thinks of his role in the saint children's loss of "purity" and his Western culture that has unwittingly contaminated that of the Mazatec. In *Transforming Modernity,* Nestor García Canclini reminds us that the world is not composed of autonomous groupings of peoples. Cultures exist within a context of local and national flows and unequal exchanges. Wasson imagines himself to have "destroyed" an Indian practice in the same vein as his counterparts, five hundred years prior, when they claimed to have "discovered" one. Canclini examines the role that Indians give to their own products as more than just passive mimicry of Western expansionist desires: "Many studies on popular cultures have started from this apocalyptic question: What can be done to stop capitalist modernization from destroying arts and crafts and other traditional expressions? Before searching for an answer, one must ask whether the question has been properly framed. It is necessary to rethink it from the perspective of a more complex notion of how the prevailing mode of production reproduces and renews its hegemony."[18] In Sabina's riddles, Wasson imposes these apocalyptic questions, but perhaps there is room to approach the ritual from a different perspective—one that acknowledges its counterhegemonic implications. Even though the niños santos are increasingly absorbed by Western markets, their sale and distribution are just as illegal as ever, reminding us that their consumption continues to be an act with subversive implications. They compel the one who eats them to see the world through a different set of eyes. The chaos and clamor of the niños allow its patients to glimpse an alternative universe, to question the existing one, and thus to privilege Fanon's zone of occult instability where new understandings of identity may emerge.

Sabina's contribution to bringing Huautla to the global marketplace is told in the preface of *María Sabina: Her Life and Chants*. Here we can glean a preliminary notion of the Western values associated with Mazatec "selling out." Author Jerome Rothenberg describes María Sabina's far-reaching fame, then takes pains to defend or juxtapose this commercial and cultural acclaim with her adherence to a traditional Mazatec lifestyle:

> I hope, in calling attention to the degree of fame that she has, that I don't frustrate the reader's enthusiasm for things Indian and remote. She's certainly aware of being famous ("the Judge knows me, the Government knows me," she sings), though by our standards it has little effect on her life *per se*. She lives still in her old tin-roofed house—though a new pre-fabricated home supplied by the government is going up nearby. She still walks barefoot up the hillside, still speaks Mazatec not Spanish, still cures and shamanizes, still smokes cigarettes and drinks beer from the bottle, still celebrates her own life of labor and her ability to make a clean bed, along with those other powers, language foremost among them, that have won her local and international repute.[19]

It is revealing to note what associations persist in Rothenberg's inventory of Sabina's "authenticity." She lives under a tin roof, walks barefoot, does not speak a European language, and apparently celebrates her ability to make a bed. She obeys the colonial imperative of the Indian who knows her place, and she correctly maintains a picturesque poverty for all (spiritual tourists) to observe. It is important to emphasize how little she profits and how remote she continues to be, or, in

Rothenberg's words, "Indian and remote," so that the money invested in pursuit of the "authentic" will not have been wasted.

On my visits, I came into contact with a person from Mexico City who was disgusted that youths greet the arriving buses and ask tourists if they want to have a ceremony. A group from Luxembourg was indignant when they found that the mushroom that grows in the Sierra Mazateca was the same species that could be acquired in the greenhouses of their homeland, and declared that their trip to eat peyote with the "Huicholes," realized five days prior, had been much more authentic. A Japanese couple, after their ceremony had already been performed, flatly refused to pay for it. These tourists go to Huautla and then are dismayed that the town is ready for them. They leave imagining that there is nothing in Huautla left to learn.

A less paternal assessment of the shaman's role in the global community is found in Richard Schechner's *Performance Theory,* in which he proposes that every performance demonstrates properties of both efficacy and entertainment. Ritual represents the efficacious end of the continuum, while theater constitutes entertainment. Agustina Martinez is willing to provide the ceremony for visitors who may not know how to respect their hostess and her customs, but she does this without removing it from the context of the sacred. The ceremony she provides is not construed by her or by her clients as "entertainment." In many ways the Western gaze has replaced the Mexica and the Spanish empires and exacts a tribute from the Mazatecs of both spiritual commodity *and* authenticity. On the one hand, adventurers who are richer in information and property than the Mazatec demand a level of primitivism from their hosts to justify their having invested in the visit. On the other hand, the division of entertainment and efficacy regarding the consumption of the mushroom has created a demand for the psilocybin that divorces it from its sacred context and places it in the environment of the laic drug trip at the entertainment end of the continuum.

Indigenous curatives come into dialogue with Western consumer tendencies, but these exchanges do not need to signal the end of their medicinal and spiritual efficacy. In Wasson's scenario, another Columbus accidentally stumbles onto a populated continent. What he gleaned of native speech tells us more about his own desires than about a ceremony that alters states and regards the Western "I" as pathology rather than vantage point.

Information for Tourists

The exchange of Mazatec spiritual practice for the tourist dollar, and the consumption of traditional folk remedies by Western seekers, does not have to imply the subordination of the Sierra Mazateca to Western imperialism. Fears of the millennial marketplace and the new world order are uncannily similar to the pre-Aristotelian voices that insisted that the world was flat, and that a vessel guided far enough into the ocean's expanse would eventually fall over the edge. While some of this alarm can be healthy, the vision seems to deny the existence of efficacious resistance fronts or, quite possibly, is incapable of recognizing them when they do occur. Traditional Mesoamerican women healers resist Western conceptions of self and community, and by investing in indigenous curatives, nonlocal patronage helps Mazatec people remain in their homeland, rather than being forced to emigrate and abandon the lands that represent not just their food, but an entire agricultural universe that is the symbolic center of Mazatec identity.

The exchange of money for ritual means that nonlocal currency is now a factor in the economic determination of Mazatecs and might be harming their traditional way of life. But the intervention of spiritual tourism that connects Western and Indian products works within a complex fabric of global transactions in which the specific case of mushroom tourism may constitute a way to guard against the invasion of modern manufacture and capitalist modes of crop cultivation.

The mushroom as commodity fetish frightens the cultural purist who, as Canclini points out, conceives world cultures as separate but equal autonomous units for which exchange constitutes a departure from the norm. The reality is that we are, and have long been, interconnected. The flow of specific fetishes does not guarantee their consecration—or their desecration. Tomlinson describes the tenor of much globalization theory in his section entitled "Nightmares: Global Culture as Cultural Imperialism." He agrees that theories of cultural imperialism represent some of the earliest theories of cultural globalization but also cautions us against the reduction of culture to its consumption of (regularly North American) material goods.

> Examples of global brands and mass-cultural icons have indeed become clichés—Coke, McDonald's, Calvin Klein, Microsoft,

> Levi's, Dallas, IBM, Michael Jackson . . . some even becoming synonyms for Western cultural hegemony itself: "McWorld" (Barber 1995), "Coca-colization" (Howes 1996), "McDonaldization" (Ritzer 1993) and even "McDisneyization" (Ritzer and Liska 1997). . . . The problem with the cultural imperialism argument is that it merely assumes such a penetration: it makes a leap of inference from the simple presence of cultural goods to the attribution of deeper cultural or ideological effects. . . . Culture simply does not transfer in this unilinear way.[20]

Tomlinson warns against the conflation of cultural identity and consumption, reminding us that the purchase of Western products does not necessarily define how a group imagines itself.

In the realm of personal experience, I do not think that I cast myself in terms of my consumer status. Growing up, I never felt that the presence of the Japanese vehicle in the family garage meant that "our people" were expelled from the garden of ethnic purity. My mother's Datsun, with the awful cream-colored paint job covering up the factory forest green, was just as Mexican American as a vintage Chevy or a lowered El Dorado. The option of buying a vehicle "made by purebred Aztecs out of alloys produced in Aztlán" simply did not exist. (There is, however, a one-hundred-spoke wheel called the "Azteca.") Am I what I buy? My consumer relationship to the world rises out of a complex set of conditions and is not articulated in my mind as a unilateral attack of the "foreign" on the "local."

There are other cautions against imagining globalization as total and inevitable cultural imperialism that we should consider in relation to the Sierra Mazateca. While the spectacle of tourists flocking to Huautla de Jiménez occasions the transformation of Mazatec rituals, the interests of transnational corporations such as commercial farming result in investments that force Mazatecs out of the mountains altogether. Economic conditions that abet the persistence of family maize plots and that foster pride in indigenous customs tend to mediate some of the aspects of alienation that, as Marx points out, are the very definition of wage-laborers in a capitalist society. Having an income that bolsters the local economy allows people to continue to be *shuta enima*—workers of the mountain. When tourism brings economic resources to the mountain, it enables the continuity of

Mazatec livelihood in the highlands, which is at the core of their conception of being.

In the case of Huautla, the influx of outsiders and their currency may in fact constitute a source of cohesion that allows shamans and their communities to continue to survive economically in the highlands and to conserve what Eckart Boege considers to be the central paradigm in Mazatec identity: the cultivation of maize.

> Según el anciano Ramos, ser *shuta enima* implica trabajar en el monte. Quisiera resaltar como problema lo que significa trabajo para la creación de la identidad. Se trata de la transformación de la naturaleza—el monte—con la acción humana. El nosotros trabajamos—aun cuando sembrar sea a veces una acción individual—tiene detrás de sí la aldea o las aldeas.[21]
>
> [According to the elder Ramos, to be *shuta enima* implies one who works in the mountain. I would like to emphasize the manner in which the problem of work relates to the construction of identity. It is based on the transformation of nature—the mountain—by means of human action. The "we work," even when sowing seeds is sometimes an individual action, has the village or villages behind it.]

Thus, the cultivation of maize and the transformation of the mountains into human sustenance are the organizing principles of the community—the very center of how Mazatecs understand self, being, and nature. There is no "we" without implying the work performed on the mountain.

The majority of the Mazatec population depends on subsistence-level farming, with the family plot providing not only daily sustenance, but also the fabric of social cohesion. The increasing necessity to plant only one crop, according to the demands of the market economy, is displacing the complex relationship between Mazatecs and their ecosystems, even contributing to their demise. Changes brought about by privatization threaten the balance between Mazatecs and their traditional relationship with their ecosystem. In the 1950s, 22,000 Mazatecs had to leave their homes. With the presence of the newly established Miguel Alemán Company, they lost 500 square kilometers—one half of their arable lands in the lower part of their territory. This displacement reduces the traditional cycles of clearing and burning, and leaves younger generations with no choice but to abandon their region temporarily or permanently to perform commercial farm labor (such as Loma Bonita in the pineapple crop, or in the cane and sugar fields) or to set out in the direction of Mexico City.[22]

To envision the presence of nonlocal currency in the Sierra Mazateca as the apocalypse reduces the complexities of Mazatec survival and determination to a few points of convergence with Western assailants. When shuta enima are forced to leave the mountain, there is no longer a name for their being. By creating an atmosphere of economic determination that collaborates with spiritual tourism, wise men and women bring capital to their homes, and they can continue to work the mountain.

The idea that tourism can be life-giving is not a new one. Author and performance artist Guillermo Gómez-Peña makes a similar case in his treatment of "Zapatourismo" (tourism to visit the Zapatistas) in Chiapas, where radicals from around the globe flock to participate in indigenous insurgencies. In his performances, Gómez-Peña creates multivalent hypertypes (a word I am using to describe the exaggerated stereotypes he uses in his performances) to call attention to the problem of how the Western perceiver interacts with indigenous and mestizo peoples of the Americas. The characters that he and his cohorts enact are a critique of where we position ourselves. His characters' names clown with the juxtaposition of first and third world roles. Gomez-Peña has performed as the Supernintendo Ranchero, Border Brujo, El Warrior for Gringostroika, El Untranslatable Vato, El Aztec High-Tech, El Naftazteca, El Mexterminator, El Mad Mex, Information Superhighway Bandito, and El Web-back. His companion in arms, Roberto Sifuentes, has been a CyberVato in a television experiment, and another collaborator, James Luna, has worked with him in an ongoing series of actions entitled "The Shame-man Meets El Mexican't at the Smithsonian Motel and Golf Course." The names of Gómez-Peña's hypertypes do not resist the trappings of our modern era, but rather seek them out and wrestle with them in the transnational circus ring. His work insists that cultural blending is the normative experience of the borderlands, which is less a geographic line in the dirt than it is a frame of mind. We carry our borders with us and impose them on those we meet. We make decisions based on preconceptions and first impressions about what is modern, what is archaic, and what is exotic.

A focus on tourism that denies the complex process of positionality serves to naturalize Western imperialism instead of neutralizing its consequences. However, an approach to tourism that embraces its complexity and uses points of geographical convergence to question colonization's axioms can have liberatory implications. I might also mention that this is difficult in practice, as Gómez-Peña remarks below. On his trip to San Cristóbal de las Casas, realized in the first years following the 1995 Zapatista uprising in the same city, Gómez-Peña and his performance team traveled to Zapatista-controlled territories in Chiapas. His performance notes are published in *Dangerous Border Crossers* (2000), where he confesses to his reservations about participating in "radical tourism."

> Since the mid-80s I have created performances and installations dealing with the commodification and exoticization of ethnicity by the tourist and the pop culture industries. Perhaps because of this I am overly cautious about performing the involuntary role of stupid tourist myself. I particularly distrust the type of tourism which promises a more "meaningful," "fair," and "radical" exchange of political ideas and cultural experiences, which of course, rarely happens.[23]

The tone of distrust shifts to outright disdain as the author reflects on the presence of nonlocal participants in the Chiapanecan town, thoroughly converting it into a theme park of auto-exoticism for the purpose of captivating foreign imaginations and meeting foreign desires. Calling it the "SoHo of indigenismo," Gómez-Peña describes the presence of cappuccino bars, taco restaurants with revolutionary names, radical tourists such as latter-day hippies, macho journalists, anthropologists, and burnt-out leftists seeking the solution to their postcolonial angst.

The "zapatour" is not complete without the exchange of cultural secrets, romantic interludes with Indian-looking "others," and authentic guides to take them through the jungle while exchanging radicalisms and cheap tequila. Gómez-Peña is clearly disappointed with this panorama of hungry identity seekers who look to assuage colonial guilt with the price of an airline ticket. Hence, his conclusion in which he gives a hearty commendation of the experience is surprising.

> Paradoxically, this revolutionary fiesta is perhaps one of the main reasons why the Mexican government hasn't exterminated the Zapatistas. In the suspicious eyes of the government (Mexican politicians are very sensitive to international public opinion), each tourist, specially those with foreign names and video cameras, becomes a potential witness; a probable reporter. Because of this, I support it wholeheartedly . . . and even promote it among my gringo friends: "Go to Chiapas. Buy lots of trinkets. Wear a Zapatista mask. Dance and drink. Have lots of sex with an activist. Pay lots of money for the zapatour. It's worth it. You might be contributing indirectly to the survival of Zapatismo.[24]

As Gómez-Peña suggests, the presence of tourists in one of the Western Hemisphere's most highly militarized regions may be preventing the next full-scale massacre of Mexico's indigenous peoples and shielding their routes of resistance from the hostile national paradigm.

In a national environment that systematically silences and effaces the contributions of Mesoamerican civilizing projects, indigenous groups that participate in the spirit of defiance have their own strategies and negotiations of ethnicity and national participation. Looking at its multivalent implications, Gómez-Peña comes to terms with the fact that non-Indians and foreign participants who travel to the Chiapanecan jungle and highlands are not only spectators, but actors as well. Both indigenous and exogenous parties perform ethnicity and create spectacle with this postmodern interplay of cultures.

For tourism as progressive action to take place, visitors to Huautla de Jimenez may want to think about how business acumen among Mazatecs does not need to denote the devastation of indigenous philosophy. We must creatively challenge the misconceived Western nostalgia for an imagined time when "they" acted less like "us." While it is acceptable in capitalist society for acquisition to be an end in itself—and this is perceived as a virtue even when acquisition far surpasses economic need—if Indians display signs of the individual accumulation of wealth, they are summarily dismissed by Western travelers, academic and otherwise, as being spoiled and "inauthentic." In other words, Western pursuit of profit and fetishism is rational. Indian and mestizo self-preservation and adaptation are framed as avarice and betrayal.

Conclusion

Reflecting on Frantz Fanon's four proposed stages in the development of revolutionary culture, I introduced my relationship to Mazatec shamanism as one that was initially grounded in the second stage, in which those aspiring to decolonial thought production try to allay the consequences of colonization by celebrating what is "essential" in their own culture. My own essentialization of Chicana identity led me to pursue contact with indigenous shamanism as a curative for colonial thinking, imagining that I would find clues about my heritage in the lost or stolen lore of Mesoamerica. I did not find a quick fix for my fugue state. Instead, I had to come to terms with the realization that Anahuac was not a location or a symbol, but a zone of occult instability where the fugue itself was a condition of participation. Looking for "the Indian way," I found the shaman Agustina Martinez, who was every bit a businesswoman and participant in the circumstances of our time.

By exploring the implications of globalization in the highlands of Oaxaca, it becomes clear that Western modernity has little tolerance for traditional communities that adapt to meet the exigencies of the global marketplace. For Mesoamerican women, globalization and indigeneity present specific problems. Feminist scholars have observed that Indian women who are locally and nationally disenfranchised can gain access to greater autonomy in transnational settings. María Sabina and Agustina Martinez are two examples of women who share Mazatec shamanism with the twenty-first century. If such women do not adapt their abilities to meet transnational possibilities, then shamanism will remain frozen behind the glass pane of a museum diorama, forever administering the same medicine to the same patient suffering from the same eternal malady. However, the mushroom ritual does not languish behind a hermetically sealed divide—it interacts with today's world, with all of its ethical challenges and complexities.

6

Contesting the Pathogen Myth

Chicano Literature as Curative

> If undocumented border-crossers are depicted as pathogens entering the bloodstream of the nation, then immigrants are not seen as people to be treated for disease but as things to be treated against.[1]
>
> —*María Ruiz*

The Pathogen Myth

MESOAMERICAN LABOR AND MESOAMERICAN SILENCE are a lucrative combination, as the myth of the Mexican-as-pathogen dehumanizes Latino immigrants, thus creating a climate that tolerates abuses of the immigrant labor force. At the foundation of US labor history, slavery and indentured servitude brought wealth to the elite. When slavery was abolished, color lines continued to demarcate the privileged from the underserved, with Jim Crow and other segregation laws ensuring that elites maintained the social- and class-based privileges to which they believed they were entitled. Child labor and immigrant labor helped fill in where there was a dearth of native-born people of color. The technology of dehumanizing a given population is no recent phenomenon, but rather arrived on boats from Europe as part of its charter mythology: one people was chosen by God to bring civilization to the rest, and it is an act of charity to permit those who are less than chosen to work for those who are closer to God. For politicians, corporations, and households to call an immigrant group "alien" is to ensure that a subhuman, retrograde population will perform the most undesirable labor in a way that constructs the employer as a benevolent agent of charity. First slaves, then children and immigrants—the disenfranchisement of US workers has been accomplished through the pathogen myth that screams racial epithets in an attempt to drown out the tragic dirge that is this country's labor history.

Xenophobic sentiments are particularly invested in demonizing the border crossings of Spanish-speaking women. In "Border Narratives, HIV/AIDS, and Latina/o Health in the United States: A Cultural Analysis," María Ruiz writes that among white supremacist "nativists," the danger of female border crossers from Mexico ultimately resides in their fertility. The pregnant woman represents the embodiment of the multiplying brown menace. Ruiz' image and ensuing quote below articulate the fear of brown women's fertility and address the graphic location of the Spanish-speaking mother in the center of the highway sign (fig. 6.1). In the middle of the placard, Ruiz points out that while English-speakers are warned against the illegal threat of this

Figure 6.1 Caution/Prohibido sign on Interstate 5, San Diego County, California

depicted family (caution, beware), the Spanish-speakers are told "*prohibido*" (prohibited).

> Just as animals are thought to be drawn to cross the road either by ignorance or natural instinct, so too, this sign implies, are undocumented crossers. The man–woman–child image represents a family of "illegal aliens" but also the Latino family, equally imprinted with the border. Though the sign may function to warn highway drivers of undocumented immigrants' perilous efforts to cross on foot areas restricted to cars, the conservative political impetus behind the sign equates the man-woman-child image with a functioning reproductive unit, and the sign itself as a prohibition of unauthorized breeding (an antifamily message aimed at nonwhite families). The sign also conjures up narratives of the "illegal alien" family in flight, reckless motherhood, and danger. Framed in this way, the sign symbolizes the threat of Latino growth to the dream of the United States as purely Anglo and English-speaking. Unauthorized border crossings are dangerous, but in different ways for different people. The Latina woman is at the center of these messages, both literally and symbolically, and drags behind her a small child.[2]

Ruiz' analysis articulates the conflation of the woman migrant with excessive reproduction and invasion. Fears of uncontrolled fertility are narrated in the above image as a dangerous assault on the United States: the undesirable running bodies are flowing into the country and breeding as they come.

The forced sterilization of minority women in the later part of the twentieth century shows how urgently institutions have worked to eradicate the "infestation," as evinced by the national disposition toward Latina fertility. In 1976 the National Coalition Against Sterilization Abuse issued a statement claiming that in Los Angeles alone between 1968 and 1970, and with the help of federal funds, the number of sterilizations that were not medically necessary increased dramatically at Women's Hospital (LA County–USC Medical Center): hysterectomies shot up 742 percent; tubal ligations went up 470 percent. Additionally, 35 percent of all Puerto Rican women of childbearing age had been sterilized. The statement also affirmed that one in five married black women had been sterilized.[3]

An affidavit provided by Karen E. Benker, MD, on May 30, 1980, described the climate of the OB-GYN ward at the Women's Hospital during the radical upswing in sterilizations. On her first day in the obstetrics ward, Benker listened as the department's director, Dr. Edward J. Quilligan, "announced proudly that they had recently received a grant from the federal government for, I believe, $2,000,000.00, 'to see how low we can cut the Negro and Mexican birth rate in the country.'" Benker's affidavit reads:

> On almost a daily basis I saw the following types of coercion being used: the doctor would hold a syringe in front of the mother who was in labor pain and ask her if she wanted a pain killer; while the woman was in the throes of a contraction the doctor would say, "Do you want the pain to stop? Do you want to have to go through this again? Sign the papers." Women who were having difficulties were told that they would die if they had any more children; this was seldom true. . . . Another method of coercion that I saw several times was to give a mother a shot of Valium intravenously as preparation for the operation and then thrust the consent forms under her hand so that she would be too groggy to resist or be aware of what she was signing.[4]

Benker recalled one occasion in which a doctor simply added the words "tubal ligation" underneath the C-section consent form after the mother had already signed. A more typical manner of obtaining the consent form was by having the nurse silently offer papers to the laboring mother who signed unquestioningly. The sterilization would then be performed by a resident doctor.

According to Benker, the atmosphere of the OB-GYN ward at the Los Angeles County–University of Southern California Medical Center was one of intense distress. The constant screams of women in labor met with harsh fluorescent lighting and a harried staff with students and doctors going without sleep for entire twenty-four-hour periods. On two occasions, Benker recalled, laboring women were slapped by staff "to make them shut up." This scenario was nothing less than terrifying, but even more so for the Spanish-speaking women in labor experiencing emotional distress, physical suffering, and the additional vulnerability of not understanding the procedures being performed on their bodies.[5]

The explanations for why so many women were sterilized were fairly consistent. One of the attending staff told a group of medical students, "We're doing the coons like we do back home" (that is, down South). Doctors often complained that women who did not speak English were not really "American" and that they had come from Mexico pregnant on the bus just so that they could have their baby born a US citizen "so they can't be deported themselves." The civil suit for damages filed by ten victims of coerced sterilization was entitled *Dolores Madrigal, et al., versus E. J. Quilligan, et al.* The Honorable Jesse W. Curtis ruled against the plaintiffs and in favor of Quilligan and his staff, thereby legitimizing the doctors' actions in performing nonconsensual sterilizations of Mexican women.[6]

Mexican American authors are acutely aware of the pathogen myth and its impact on Latina and Chicana womanhood. Collaborating with the political project of decolonization, their protagonists reside on land that was Indian before it was Spanish, and Mexican before it was usurped by Anglo Americans; yet the women in the novels I discuss in this chapter must constantly face symbolic and explicit hostilities challenging their presence in this country. As they dwell in locales named for Mexican settlers on streets with Spanish names in states whose first constitutions were drafted in Spanish, they confront the accusations that Mexican women are pathogens—allegations that are felt at every institutional and informal level of US society. The woman healer in Mexican American arts thus constitutes an emblem that refutes the infestation model of Mexican womanhood by recovering its Mesoamerican physicians—women that have engaged in a historical and spiritual relationship with the natural environment of the Americas long before the arrival of Europeans.

In Rudolfo Anaya's *Bless Me, Ultima* (1971), Ana Castillo's *So Far from God* (1993), and Luis Alberto Urrea's *The Hummingbird's Daughter* (2005), the figure of the Mesoamerican wise woman alleviates the physical and spiritual sufferings of her charges. Anaya's character Ultima helps her young apprentice to interpret the ecological world as the foundation of wellness. Castillo's Caridad, as in the genre of Spanish hagiography, represents the fusion of Iberian martyrdom and the iconography of radical Chicana feminism. In Urrea's novel, Teresita's tale reclaims the oppressed dark-skinned womanhood that is so often represented as disposable in the colonial imagination, identifying

Teresita's curative abilities as the manifestation of Mesoamerican ways of knowing. Each of these characters contests the pervasive Mexican-as-pathogen narrative by honoring the transmission of Mesoamerican curatives as an epistemological project.

Chicano Literature as Anti-Oppression Writing

The cultural innovators of the early Chicano movement (1965–75) created literary works that were a form of social protest against the violence of poverty and ethnic discrimination. In New Mexico, the state in which two of the novels discussed in this chapter are set, the post–World War II time period drew the parameters of national inclusion along color lines: Mexican war veterans could not join the local American Legion post; Mexicans were barred from the more affluent restaurants, shops, hotels, and entertainment venues in the Anglo-dominant eastern part of the state; schools and churches were separate for white and brown children and congregations; and sororities and fraternities at the University of New Mexico did not allow Mexican Americans to become members. Nearly 97 percent of the Mexicans in New Mexico were US-born, and they constituted about half the population of their state, but this did not prevent them from being treated as second-class citizens in their homeland.[7]

The Mexican American GI generation exposed the frailty of US claims of democracy and equality. After earning outstanding records of military service, they came home where their people were being treated as the enemy. Recessions in 1949 and in the early part of the 1950s catalyzed nativist fears of the undocumented worker, culminating in Operation Wetback, a large-scale roundup spearheaded by retired generals who viewed Mexicans as war criminals.[8]

During the war period, undocumented immigration had been encouraged, in order to meet the needs of agricultural and war-related industries as well as active military duty. Large-scale attacks on Mexican Americans known as the zoot suit riots, Operation Wetback, and the exclusion of veterans of Mexican descent from public institutions along with other flagrant forms of discrimination and hate all precipitated the anger and confrontational demeanor of the 1960s Chicano movement.

The Chicano movement employed nationalism and separatism as strategies of resistance. The intensity of poverty and racism during the 1960s ignited many cities, turning them into hotbeds of open aggression. The death toll of these urban rebellions illustrates the scope of human desperation that minorities experienced. Between 1965 and 1969 riots in Watts left thirty-five dead; forty-three died in Detroit, and Newark, New Jersey, saw twenty-six fatalities. The civil rights era gave a voice, and a set of practical approaches, to the outrage of US people of color. When a galvanized group of Mexican Americans ushered in a new era of social transformation, provocateurs and informants working for local and federal law enforcement agencies infiltrated Chicano movement groups. The militarized environment of identity politics was fueled by the high-stakes circumstances in which Mexican Americans voiced their demands.

Just as African Americans had reclaimed the derogatory expression "black" and transformed it to represent ethnic pride, Mexican Americans took hold of the pejorative term "Chicano" and turned it into an emblem of self-worth. From the days of colonization, when the Spaniards had shortened the word "Mexicano" to "Chicano" as an insult to Mexican Indians, the expression had held a negative connotation. However, for the generation of 1960s Mexican activists, this term exemplified the survival of indigeneity despite the violence of centuries of colonization. To be a Chicano or a Chicana was to be proud of one's Indian roots and critical of the oppressive forces that vilified the legacy of Mesoamerican and North American Indians and mestizos.

The early Chicano movement focused on a range of issues, including economic self-determination, social justice, access to education, and political representation. Various organizations dedicated themselves to these aims. The United Farm Workers Union, led by César Chavez and Dolores Huerta; the Chicano student movement that created Movimiento Estudiantil Chicano de Aztlán (MEChA); the New Mexico land grant movement championed by Reies Lopez Tijerina; the Colorado Crusade for Justice, led by Rudolfo "Corky" Gonzalez, Ricardo V. Cruz, and Católicos por la Raza; the militant Brown Berets that styled themselves in the spirit of the African American Black Panthers; and the Raza Unida Party were each significant in raising awareness and provoking change.

Unlike the Mexican American organizations of the 1950s such as the League of United Latino Citizens (LULAC) and the GI Forum, which both sought greater levels of cooperation and inclusion within US institutions, the 1960s organizers expressed the desire to break from the mainstream and embrace the politics of the street in order to do so. Marches, boycotts, hunger strikes, high school and college walkouts, verbal and physical confrontations, civil disobedience, and other forms of protest characterized the nationalistic Chicano agenda.

Essentialism was both a result and a strategy of the early movement to counter the hostility that its actors endured. Mexican American organizers were profoundly aware of the fatalities and the military occupations of black ghettoes during the Watts, Detroit, and Newark revolts. Their ranks were jeopardized by local and federal surveillance. The practices of Chicano activists made the movement's members easy targets of prejudice. Chicano movement politics included the tactic of separatism to uphold and protect its values and integrity, but also to ward against the felt threat of outside agents capable of dismantling their cause from within. The ramifications of being fired, imprisoned, or killed compelled movement leaders to reject discourses that did not appeal to their strident militarism.

Feminism was just such a perceived threat to the integrity of the early movement. The women's movement, spearheaded in large part by middle-class Anglo Americans, did not seem compatible with the struggles of poor Mexican Americans who were coping with issues of racial, economic, and cultural forms of oppression.[9] At least this was the message that many Chicano men conveyed to their female counterparts, who worked just as hard as the men but were awarded fewer positions of leadership and representation within the movement's operations. Branded as "women's libbers" and "agringadas" (white-identified women), the early movement feminists raised women's issues and called for an end to gender-specific tasks, facing ridicule by their peers in response to their views.[10] Articulated as the dialectic between "feminists" and "loyalists," Chicanas as well as Chicanos disagreed with a feminist agenda, declaring that the enemy was the "gabacho"—not the macho.[11] A "liberated woman" seemed antithetical to the "traditional" cultural values that the Chicano movement sought to defend.[12] The problem for Chicana feminists, then, was to develop a program that asserted their agency without turning their backs on cultural identity and community cohesion.

By the mid-1970s Mexican American leadership was being co-opted by government and private institutions that responded to the movement's demands for increased political representation, but did this by picking the more mutable delegates from the Latino population. The militancy that characterized the early movement gave way to a growing wave of Mexican American professionals that proposed change from within the system. A movement that had previously preached separatism and nationalism now saw its more moderate leaders seeking inclusion through upward mobility. Unlike the "Chicanos," this post-movement group of US Latinos/as relied on institutional interests instead of community needs to maintain their status. The term *Hispanic* allowed for the homogenization of all US Latino groups under one category that privileges Iberian over Mesoamerican ancestry. The Chicano movement espoused radicalism, while the era of Nixon and its successors preferred the more pliable, less confrontational denotation *Hispanic*.

As a result of the movement, today many universities, colleges, and cultural centers promote a more plural definition of US Latino experience. The critique of the imprint of the US–Mexico border, bi- and multilingualism, feminist and queer discourses, and new information technologies all collaborate to privilege more diverse perspectives on Latino and Chicano progressive agendas. The Chicano movement, with its power handshake, MEChA hand-clap (beginning in unison at a slow pace, the public builds a steadily quickening crescendo of applause), and playlist of Mexican ballads and lowrider rhythm-and-blues songs are remembered with affection and respect in today's Mexican American forums but are seldom privileged as workable models for grassroots activism.

In Chicano and Chicana literature, Mesoamerican knowledge has long held a prominent position. Following the historiography of Luis Leal, who argues resolutely for the inclusion of the early periods (just as American literature includes the colonial period as part of its legacy), we can point to Cabeza de Vaca's narrative as the first instance of Indian healing in Mexican American literature.[13] Álvaro Núñez Cabeza de Vaca's *Relación de los naufragios* (1542) not only provides us with a foundational text in the history of US–Mexican literature but also constitutes the first literary treatment of curanderismo.

Cabeza de Vaca's story begins when Pánfilo de Narváez and approximately four hundred men set out in 1527 from Cuba to explore the southeast coast of the United States from Florida to the Rio Grande. A violent storm shipwrecked the group off the coast of what is now Texas, where few survivors managed to struggle to shore. A Spanish military official named Álvaro Núñez Cabeza de Vaca was among these survivors. During the next ten years Cabeza de Vaca and his fellow survivors ventured overland through much of what is today the southwest United States. They eventually reached Mexico City, which was by then the seat of New Spain's power in the Americas. The following excerpt documents Álvaro Núñez Cabeza de Vaca's initial reaction to native healers he encountered on his ill-fated voyage with the Narváez expedition.

> What the physician does is to make some incisions where the sick person has pain, and then sucks all around them. They perform cauterizations with fire, which is a thing among them considered to be very effective, and I have tried it and it turned out well for me. And after this, they blow upon the area that hurts, and with this they believe that they have removed the malady. The manner in which we performed cures was by making the sign of the cross over them and blowing on them, and praying a Pater Noster and an Ave Maria, and as best we could, beseeching our Lord God that he grant them health and move them to treat us well. Our Lord God in his mercy willed that all those on whose behalf we made the supplication, after we had made the sign of the cross over them, said to others that they were restored and healthy, and on account of this they treated us well, and refrained from eating in order to give their food to us, and they gave us skins and other things. (115)

Cabeza de Vaca's narrative provides a window onto the early formation of spiritual and medical authority in today's US Southwest. At first he and his Spanish companions sustain the European view of professionalized medicine, in which a diploma confers the status of medical authority and in which medicine and religion constitute discrete fields of specialization. Next, the narrator is forced to perform indigenous cures owing to these extenuating circumstances: he must comply with his native hosts in order to eat. Quickly he is converted to their methods when he has experienced empirical knowledge of their efficacy. Then he adjusts his practices to allow for his own system of beliefs, combining the techniques of the native medical authorities with Christian prayers. Cabeza de Vaca's transculturation process is the earliest example of a performed mestizo knowledge base.

The pre-Hispanic period (before 1527), the Spanish period (until 1821), and the Mexican period (until 1848) were followed by what some literary historians consider to be the beginning of Chicano literature, since the modern border between Mexico and the United States as well as the imposition of English as the dominant language created a new political identity for Americans of Mexican descent. Luis Leal, Philip Ortego, Ray Paredes, and Amelia María de la Luz Montes are among the notable literary historians to have documented and examined this stage of literary production. From this period, María Amparo Ruiz de Burton was the first Mexican American author in the United States to write novels in English. Ruiz de Burton wrote two novels, *Who Would Have Thought It?* (1872) and *The Squatter and the Don* (1885), under the pseudonym C. Loyal.

The Chicano contemporary period began around 1965. In 1967 Quinto Sol was established in Berkeley, California, making this the first Mexican American publishing house. Four years later, the Premio Quinto Sol was awarded to Rudolfo Anaya for *Bless Me, Ultima*, and the work instantly became a cornerstone of the Chicano movement's literary canon. Along with Ultima, curanderos have appeared consistently in the creative works of the contemporary period. Luís Valdez's popular film *La Bamba* (1987) emphasizes Ritchie Valens's trip to Mexico and ensuing encounter with a shaman as the crux of his spiritual awakening. This meeting between the US-born musician and the Mexican healer anticipates not only Ritchie's rise to fame, but his plummet to an untimely death. It is with the shaman that he learns to cope with his recurring nightmare in which he sees himself fall from the sky. When he dies in an airplane crash, his fate is already foreshadowed by this scene in which he comes to terms with his musical—and mortal—destiny. The moment with the shaman in which fears are abated and life, death, vocation, and the shaman's journey are all syncopated, and Ritchie's brother sums up this simultaneity of experience by turning to him to declare, "*This* is Mexico."

Alfredo Vea's *La Maravilla* tells the coming-of-age story of a young boy who is raised by a Spanish curandera grandmother and Yaqui Indian grandfather in the Southwest. Leslie Marmon Silko's 1991 novel *Almanac of the Dead* involves native women on the path to restoring Indian lands to their original custodians. In George Lopez's stand-up routine he mentions Mexican Americans and health care, pointing out that the neighborhood curandera's methods are much more accessible to poor Mexicans who must simply "live with shit wrong."

The Mazatec shaman María Sabina is included in the four-storey-high, Woman's Building mural entitled *Maestrapeace* in San Francisco, California, and Guillermo Gómez-Peña creates the spectacle of New World "shamanism" in his performance art. Carmen Lomas Garza's painting entitled *Curandera* interprets the occasion in which a healer performed several cleansings for her sister to help her overcome some of her adolescent rebelliousness. Gloria Anzaldúa's bilingual children's book *Prietita and the Ghost Woman/Prietita y la Llorona* (1996) is a fiction work describing a young girl's apprenticeship to the local curandera, who serves as the medical authority of the community; likewise, her seminal, genre-bending autobiography entitled *Borderlands/La Frontera* associates the act of writing with shamanism, as writers are mediators between worlds, shape-shifting to provide the words of healing that restore balance and light. In short, even a much-abbreviated list of healers in contemporary Mexican American cultural production permits us to appreciate the breadth and persistence of curanderos in Chicano arts and letters. This figure is too widely depicted to survey here; rather, I have selected three novels in which the curandera establishes the centrality of Mesoamerican knowledge. Consistent in each of these works is the female healer who inverts the Mesoamerican-woman-as-pathogen narrative by celebrating its opposite; Mesoamerican women of knowing are the cure.

Bless Me, Ultima and the Diversity of Metaphysical Possibility

When José Vasconcelos coined "*la raza cósmica*" (the cosmic race) in 1925, he conjured the notion of a shining, predestined amalgam of world cultures, but his optimistic phrasing is far too bloodless to do justice to the violence of conquest. Set in the era of the Second World War, Rudolfo Anaya's novel *Bless Me, Ultima* (1971) is told by an adult narrator recalling the days of his early childhood. Antonio Márez is the novel's young protagonist, who serves as a metaphor of mestizo identity, narrated here as the crisis of metaphysical possibilities. Neither a melting pot nor a cosmic fusion, Antonio is adrift in spiritual turmoil until Ultima arrives and turns him toward the natural world for answers.

When Ultima comes to live with Antonio's family on the outskirts of a small New Mexican town, Antonio instinctively trusts this elderly woman who moves with quiet dignity and exudes the fragrance of wild pastures. Under her tutelage, the earth is transformed into a sentient being that interacts with those who are attentive enough to hear its messages. The character Ultima helps Antonio understand that he need not turn his back on his Spanish Catholic devotions to be one with the pantheistic indigenous teachings that she imparts. For Chicano culture, Ultima is a powerful mediator between European and Mesoamerican ontologies whose teachings merge as an interstitial site of wholeness between two worlds.

In celebrating the indigenous spirituality that is a seminal aspect of the curandera's vocation, Anaya refutes the Mexican-as-pathogen mythos by linking Antonio and his heritage to the land.

> Ultima came to stay with us the summer I was almost seven. When she came the beauty of the llano unfolded before my eyes, and the gurgling waters of the river sang to the hum of the turning earth. The magical time of childhood stood still, and the pulse of the living earth pressed its mystery into my blood. She took my hand, and the silent, magic powers she possessed made beauty from the raw, sun-baked llano, the green river valley, and the blue bowl which was the white sun's home. (1)

The message that the living earth is capable of communication, and that it shares its voice with the young protagonist upon the arrival of his mysterious protectress, breaks away from the Christian vision of a nonsentient geosphere subordinate to the will of humankind. With the novel's first notes, a living earth supplants the androcentric thesis of the Christian system, in which a heavenly father shapes man, and man in turn becomes the lord of all nature. As a person imbued with greater ability to interpret the earth's voice than the protagonist, it is Ultima who represents an alternative vision of spiritual transcendence that is telluric, feminine, and indigenous, rather than celestial, patriarchal and hispanocentric.

In *The Spell of the Sensuous: Perception and Language in a More-Than-Human World* (1996), David Abram discusses the European philosophical currents that are responsible for the West's denigration of nature. Within Jewish and Christian traditions, the god exists beyond the physical reality of earth and sky, and reigns from a separate, supernatural dimension, generally conceived as a celestial one. This detachment from the earthly realm comes from the injunction to place greater store in the afterworld than the natural world, where humankind is instructed to "be fertile and increase, fill the earth and master it; and rule the fish of the sea, the birds of the sky, and all the living things that creep on earth."[14] Within the Greek philosophical tradition, Abram discusses the "estrangement from the earthly world around us" as the product of an intellectual heritage that elevates the world of ideas above the sensorial realm, where constant change is given to mean that the earthly terrain is illusory—a shadow field of tricks and deceits behind which languishes the superior plane of nonsensorial thought. The pre-European equilibrium with the native environment in the Americas was quickly toppled after conquest, and the continent that had long yielded abundance was soon poisoned and degraded by "civilization." Before the contemporary climate of Western "environmentalism," the Chicano movement had been resuscitating the voice of the natural world and honoring the indigenous elders who taught respect of the natural world as one of the most basic tenets of wisdom. With *Bless Me, Ultima,* Anaya confirms Chicano philosophy as one that ultimately belongs to a native tradition of animism, narrating this extrahuman pathway as the painful, yet necessary, revision of Christian doctrinal teachings.

Several defining conflicts unfold in the course of the protagonist's coming-of-age story involving the metaphysical possibilities that populate his boyhood universe. First, he is caught between his mother's dream for him to become a priest, and his father's desire to see his son grow into a *vaquero* and be master of lands, cattle, and horses. The conflicting desires of his mother and father represent the priorities of indigenous and Iberian cultures. Antonio's mother's surname, Luna (moon), corresponds to the native aspect of Antonio's heritage. The feminine quality of the moon as it circles the earth and the cycles by which the maternal side of his family cultivates the land represent the harmony between nature and human. María Luna and her kin wish for Antonio to conserve this peaceable life of the farmer. His father, on the other hand, is called Márez (seas) and evokes the Spanish aspect of Antonio's genealogy. Arriving from across the ocean, the conquering soldiers and settlers brought restlessness, appetite for adventure, Spanish individualism, and its inevitable companion, loneliness. Most telling is the process by which his father, a proud heir of the vaquero tradition, must give up his horse to live in town: "There was no room to keep animals in town so my father had to sell his small herd, but he would not sell his horse so he gave it to a good friend, Benito Campos. But Campos could not keep the animal penned up because somehow the horse was very close to the spirit of the man, and so the horse was allowed to roam free and no vaquero on that llano would throw a lazo on that horse" (2). The horse cannot be tamed, and the father takes to drinking and sullen moods while the animal, his wild, Iberian alter ego, roams the pastures as a solitary specter.

The contest between the Indian telluric path and the destiny of the roaming Spaniards is narrated most dramatically through Antonio's dream of the day of his birth. Anaya uses code switching seamlessly, without the benefit of italics or translations to convey the convergence of Mexican and US realities. However, Antonio's dreams are set apart in italics to introduce a different level of consciousness that is crucial to Antonio's formation. Present at his birth are representatives of both the Luna family and the Márez family.

> *We must return to the valley, the old man who led the farmers spoke. We must take with us the blood that comes after the birth. We will bury it in our fields to renew their fertility and to assure that the baby will follow our ways. He nodded for the old woman to deliver the package at the altar.*
>
> *No! the llaneros protested, it will stay here! We will burn it and let the winds of the llano scatter the ashes.*
>
> *It is blasphemy to scatter the man's blood on unholy ground, the farmers chanted. The new son must fulfill his mother's dream. He must*

> *come to El Puerto and rule over the Lunas of the valley. The blood of the Lunas is strong in him.*
>
> *He is a Márez, the vaqueros shouted. His forefathers were conquistadores, men as restless as the seas they sailed and as free as the land they conquered. He is his father's blood!*
>
> *Curses and threats filled the air, pistols were drawn, and the opposing sides made ready for battle. But the clash was stopped by the old woman who delivered the baby.*
>
> *Cease! She cried, and the men were quiet. I pulled this baby into the light of life, so I will bury the afterbirth and the cord that once linked him to eternity. Only I will know his destiny.* (6)

In between the maternal and paternal worlds is where Ultima makes her stand. It is she who connects Antonio to the earth and repairs the fissures in mestizo identity. The young boy yearns for peace between both maternal and paternal vision and discovers, under the spell of dream state, that Ultima is the key to ancestral cohesion.

Antonio is also torn between the diversity of metaphysical explanations that alternately appeal and perplex. His mother advocates the priesthood; of her four sons, he is the one she relies on to turn to books and the cloth instead of a life of guns and wanderlust. His less zealous father is also Catholic but is content to reside in the moral gray area of drunken camaraderie and the occasional visit to the women who use a red bulb for a porch light. Antonio's brothers are given to drunken or licentious behaviors that contradict the Christian doctrine that he so earnestly heeds. His friend Florence staunchly defends his schoolyard atheism, while his other friend Cico inducts him into the ancient Indian cult of the golden carp. Of the nondoctrinal beliefs to which Antonio is exposed, the sacred presence of the river, the mysterious golden carp, and Ultima's power to counteract the forces of witchcraft with her cures convey his keenest spiritual orientation throughout the text.

As with the dream state, the river's energy is privileged with italic type, as though the word itself could reach with language into another dimension, a place just beyond ordinary perception where intonations of healers and shamans reside. While gathering plant remedies, Ultima reveals that she too is aware of this murmured language that stirs in the hills.

> We were silent for a long time, lost in memories that the murmur of the mourning wind carried across the treetops. Cotton from the trees drifted lazily in the heavy air. The silence spoke, not with harsh sounds, but softly to the rhythm of our blood.
>
> "What is it?" I asked, for I was still afraid.
>
> "It is the *presence* of the river," Ultima answered.
>
> I held my breath and looked at the giant, gnarled cottonwood trees that surrounded us. Somewhere a bird cried, and up on the hill the tinkling sound of a cowbell rang. The *presence* was immense, lifeless, yet throbbing with its secret message.
>
> "Can it speak?" I asked and drew closer to Ultima.
>
> "If you listen carefully—" she whispered.
>
> "Can you speak to it?" I asked as the whirling, haunting sound touched us.
>
> "Ay, my child," Ultima smiled and touched my head, "you want to know so much."
>
> And the *presence* was gone. (42)

With this quiet induction into the world of curanderismo, Antonio learns of the spirit beings inhabiting all of nature and begins to perceive that they are possessed of a unique vocabulary that is not learned through the grammar of church or school, but in the rituals of the curandera.

If the cadence of the river's heartbeat moves fluidly into Antonio's consciousness, his discovery of the golden carp is met with real trepidation. Having learned that his is a jealous god, and that Catholic orthodoxy is the only assurance a soul can seek to avoid the eternal fires of damnation, he is certain that his wonderment at beholding the golden carp at Cico's side is sinful.

> I knew I had witnessed a miraculous thing, the appearance of a pagan god, a thing as miraculous as the curing of my uncle Lucas. And I thought, the power of God failed where Ultima's worked; and then a sudden illumination of beauty and understanding flashed through my mind. This is what I had expected God to do at my first holy communion! If God was witness to my beholding of the golden carp then I had sinned! (114)

Knowing how desperately his mother wishes for him to become a priest and rescue his sinful older brothers from eternal retribution, the unbidden reverence that springs up within him at the sight of the golden carp is a puzzle. If he is to place all faith and love in the god of the church, how can the carp so easily steal his veneration? And how can Ultima succeed at warding off the evil consequences of witchcraft where the church's holy water and the priest's blessings have failed?

While the contest between mother and father and the perplexing simultaneity of spiritual possibilities bring chaos to Antonio's inner world, dark magic is the greatest threat that looms throughout the text. This menace pursues the family in the form of Tenorio, the barber and saloonkeeper of the neighboring village, whose three daughters are skillful practitioners of witchcraft. When Antonio's uncle Lucas goes for a haircut and a drink in Tenorio's establishment, the Trementina sisters (Tenorio's three daughters) steal a lock of his hair to curse him and avenge his audacious disruption of their dark mass. Ultima cures Lucas but becomes Tenorio's enemy after releasing the innocent man from the daughters' curse. Not only does Ultima cure Lucas, but she also turns the effects of the spell back on the daughters, two of whom grow ill and eventually die. Tenorio finally manages to shoot and kill Ultima's owl that has acted as her faithful servant in the tradition of the *nagual,* or animal familiar. Although Tenorio is shot by Pedro in his act of killing the owl, Antonio understands that when the owl dies, Tenorio has succeeded in killing Ultima. She falls ill and dies shortly thereafter, bringing the novel to its conclusion.

Tenorio fears and maligns Ultima's capabilities, and the local parish authority tacitly sustains this attitude toward the nonclerical derivation of her skills. She explains the church's ambivalence toward her curatives as Antonio accompanies her to heal Lucas.

> "They let him go too long," she said, "it will be a difficult battle—"
>
> "But why didn't they call you sooner?" I asked.
>
> "The church would not allow your grandfather to let me use my powers. The church was afraid that—" She did not finish, but I knew what she would have said. The priest at El Puerto did not want the people to place much faith in the powers of la

> curandera. He wanted the mercy and faith of the church to be the villagers' only guiding light. (97)

Ultima is called in after the priests and doctors fail to achieve results, and she is finally able to cure Lucas. Her spiritual combat with Tenorio's daughters is somehow autonomous, thriving without the approval of the church, pointing to the curative efficacy of the pre-Christian, hemispheric pact of equilibrium.

Although several occasions in the novel point to Ultima's ability to reach into and adjust spiritual misalignments where doctors and priests fail, the most compelling evidence of her elevated status comes from the novel's title. Spoken from young Antonio's point of view, the title's imperative "bless me" is not directed at a priest, or at the boy's mother, from whom children in Mexican households customarily petition blessings before parting company. This blessing is a protection spell, one that creates a divine shield against evil intentions, and human and supernatural forms of malice. To ask this blessing of Ultima acknowledges that she is the immediate and final source of protection in the life of a young boy who, until coming under her tutelage, is convinced of the doctrinal dialectic of good and evil and the otherworldly conceptions of heaven and hell. After coming to revere Ultima's earth-derived system of animistic intelligence, he undergoes a profound reordering of his faith. Where once the patriarchal, exogenous priest wielded "ultimate" authority, his family's curandera now has the last word.

The efficacy of nonorthodox treatments against witchcraft and evildoing forces Antonio to admit that the church's jealous god is not the only source of miracles. The mystical murmur of the river's *presence,* the awe inspired by the golden carp, and Ultima's healing lore each serve to distance him from doctrinal puritanism. Antonio is the personification of the emerging mestizo consciousness of the Chicano movement that insisted on the inclusion of indigenous ideations of nature and being. Ultima brings Antonio to understand that these traditions are a part of him, native to his spiritual landscape because they are his heritage, too. As the embodiment of mestizo wholeness, the indigenous teachings are not to be cast aside, as the church would have done, but are a vehicle toward greater spiritual and medical alignment.

Ana Castillo and the Sacred Feminine

Ana Castillo revisits the medieval hagiographic tradition in *So Far from God*, synthesizing politics, spirituality, and medicine to craft in fictional form her project of female consciousness raising, or *concientización xicanista*. Having referred to the coerced sterilizations of the 1970s and 1980s in both the novel *The Mixquiahuala Letters* and her collection of critical essays *Massacre of the Dreamers,* Castillo counters the "Mexican woman as pathogen" stereotype in her narrative. By reappropriating hierarchical religious conventions, she constructs a woman-centered path that reinvigorates oppressed feminine forms.

So Far from God is the story of a mother, Sofia (wisdom), who bears four daughters in her marriage with Domingo. He goes from being a "Sundays only" to a completely absentee father, leaving Sofia to contend with single parenthood in the small New Mexican village of Tome. Her daughters, from oldest to youngest, are Esperanza (hope); la Loca Santa, whom family members simply call "Loca" (crazy); Caridad (charity); and Fe (faith). Along with the family, we also have the voice of the intrusive narrator. This wisecracking, omniscient observer uses colloquial language, employing the Spanish double negative in English, as when she describes Sofia's lack of social life: "No quinceñeras for none of the girls' fifteenth birthdays. Nada" (133). The casual "Spanglish" vernacular is juxtaposed with the narrator's obvious erudition, as when she compares New Mexican *santeros* (saint makers) to the "Russian monks who produced Byzantine icons" (101).

Castillo mines early Christian martyrologies for female-based cults that ennobled the wise mother and her virgin daughters. Two groups of Roman martyrs lend the main characters their names. According to *The Catholic Encyclopedia,* the fact of their existence is not questioned by historians, as descriptions of these women appear in early Greek menologies as well as in hagiographies of the Western Church. During the reign of Hadrian (AD 117–38), a Roman mother named Sophia, along with her three youthful daughters, Pistis (Faith), Elpis (Hope), and Agape (Charity), underwent martyrdom for their beliefs. They were interred on the Aurelian Way, where their remains were listed in the seventh century's *Itenerarum,* a guide to the holy places of Rome created for pilgrims. Another group of martyrs—Sapientia (Wisdom), Spes (Hope), Fides (Faith), and Caritas (Charity)—is buried on the Appian Way near the tomb of St. Cecilia. At the end of the narrative, after the deaths of Hope, Faith, and Charity, La Loca succumbs to the AIDS virus, leaving only the mother to build a female-based sacred community in spite of patriarchal law.

Unlike the essentializing tendencies of the early Chicano movement's participation in Native American Church practices, Castillo's novel does not romanticize Mexican American indigenist "tradition." For example, when the politically inclined Chicana activist Esperanza becomes involved with her movement boyfriend Rubén, Castillo is unsparing in her evaluation of early movement nationalism:

> Esperanza had been the only one to go to college. She had gotten her B.A. in Chicano Studies. During that time, she had lived with her boyfriend, Rubén (who, during the height of his Chicano cosmic consciousness, renamed himself Cuauhtemoc). This despite her mother's opposition, who said of her eldest daughter's nonsanctified union: "Why should a man buy the cow when he can have the milk for free?" "I am not a cow," Esperanza responded, but despite this, right after graduation Cuauhtemoc dumped her for a middle-class gabacha with a Corvette; they bought a house in the Northeast Heights right after their wedding. (26)

After Rubén's marriage fails, he goes back to the Native American Church and tries to rekindle his old romance with Esperanza. Although he has added a beer paunch, she still feels attracted to him and agrees to pick up where they left off: "Every two weeks she was right there with Rubén, at the teepee meetings of the Native American Church, Rubén singing and drumming, keeping the fire, watching the 'door,' teaching her the dos and don'ts of his interpretation of lodge 'etiquette' and the role of women and the role of men and how they were not to be questioned. . . ." (36). Esperanza finally manages to break off this unfulfilling romance with Rubén to take a job in Washington. Rubén had always called her a "careerist" and insisted that her professional advancement was just a sellout's route into "white" society (although he is content to have her pay their way and provide him with cash). His indigenist dogma represents a site in which indigenous and mestizo beliefs have been manipulated from within the

Chicano movement to prevent women from asserting themselves spiritually and intellectually for the sake of ethnic "preservation."

Written some twenty years after the heyday of the Chicano movement, Castillo's characters shatter the virgin/whore dichotomy by refusing to portray women as monolithic caregivers and prostitutes. Beginning with Sofia, the personification of wisdom, we observe that she is just as vulnerable to a man's persuasion as the other members of her sex. She is a savior-transformer as much as she is a great fool. By marrying Diego, she burdens herself with a self-absorbed, reckless gambler who singlehandedly wagers away the land that was her birthright. When he comes back after the daughters are already adults, she takes him back into the fold, where he proceeds to lose her last parcel of land to gambling. Despite her blind eye to his worthlessness, she manages to campaign and win the office of mayor and completely turn around the economic prospects of her town through grassroots leadership. Her capacity as sage and savior-transformer combines with foolishness as Castillo insists on the inclusion of the complexity of feminine experience in her characters.

As for the healer character of the novel, our introduction to Caridad describes a physical beauty that sets her apart from her sisters, because she looks more European than they. When her boyfriend Memo leaves her, she steers into a phase of copious drinking in which she is willing to sleep with anyone who vaguely resembles her lost Memo. This quickly earns her a "reputation" in the small, unincorporated town of Tome. When she becomes a victim of brutal rape and mutilation, save for the few beatas in town that consider her suffering to be a form of saintly martyrdom, people tacitly blame her pain on the lifestyle she has led: "But there are still those for whom there is no kindness in their hearts for a young woman who has enjoyed life, so to speak. Among them were the sheriff's deputies and the local police department; therefore Caridad's attacker or attackers were never found." (33)

When La Loca prays for her sister, she miraculously restores her body, and Caridad's spirit is wholly transformed by the nightmare and her subsequent restoration. The mutilation and recovery serve as a bridge into the next period of her life in which she becomes doña Felicia's apprentice curandera. This new stage moves her into an authority position within a female-centered spiritual practice.

Doña Felicia instructs her apprentice Caridad in the curative properties of tomatillo, sage, body massages, the occasional snort of mescal, and other remedies. Under Felicia's tutelage, Caridad's talents as a medium or channeler are soon revealed. She awakes from her first prophetic trance to report to her family that Esperanza has returned to Tome from Washington, D.C. Her second trance is a vision of her horse Corazón leading a herd of 113 horses, after which her father, Domingo, cashes in on the daily number by putting a dollar on 113.

Filling her days with tea remedies, rubdowns, and scented baths, her teacher helps Caridad to restore the internal world that had been mutilated by the attack. With Caridad's example, diverse aspects of woman all come together in one person to recover the sacred feminine. This differs from the early Chicano movement's Manichean construction of womanhood in which female agency resided in women's identification with the sanctimonious aspect of the virgin/whore dichotomy. As we see from the above passage in which feminist/loyalist allegations are implied through Rubén's disdain for Esperanza's professional empowerment, Castillo recommends a complete revision of the category of "traditional" when this is conflated with the sedimentation of el macho.

A curandera and *huesera* (bone setter), doña Felicia is the ranking official in one of the oldest New Mexican specializations. Mary Montaño writes, "The Indians of the Southwest excelled at bonesetting, and shared their knowledge with the Spanish, who called the specialists hueseros, or bonesetters. Hueseros have almost all vanished."[15] Also, female curanderismo constituted a norm in New Mexico from the time of its earliest memory: "The majority of healers in New Mexico were women. Sandra L. Stephens studied some of the letters of Nuevomexicana women of the past 150 years to learn that they discussed health quite a bit, and that they had much to face, including miscarriages, infant deaths, and epidemics of smallpox, influenza, and pneumonia. . . . Because no rural relief existed, those people were on their own."[16] Thus, in gender, age, profession and specialization, doña Felicia is firmly rooted in the local framework of medical knowledge.

After her cure, and the revelation of her talents, Caridad enters into a period of contemplative isolation on a year-long retreat in a cave. However, this is not a reference to male monastic conventions, but an echo of "Lozen, Warm Springs Apache mystic woman warrior, sister of the great chief Victorio who had vowed 'to make war against the white man forever.' And Lozen, among the last thirty-eight warriors, was the only woman" (88). She later falls in love with Esmeralda, the assistant director at the Rape Crisis Center, whose grandmother is an Acoma Pueblo Indian, and with whom she leaps over the edge of the mesa when Tsichtinako, the Pueblo Indian spirit deity that "had nourished the first two humans, who were also both female" calls to them (211).

While indigenous traditions are largely represented in a positive light in *So Far from God,* Catholicism in Castillo's mapping of Chicana consciousness is not summarily condemned for misogyny. An example of this project of recovery is found in the treatment of the Virgin of Guadalupe. Chicana feminists in particular have made a case for retaining the Virgen de Guadalupe as the patroness of Chicana liberation. In *Massacre of the Dreamers,* Castillo writes, "The Virgin of Guadalupe is a favorite. She is not only the patron saint of México, a cultural bond for all of us as 'Guadalupanas,' but also the 'brown' mother goddess, Tonantzin. She, therefore, is an ancient indigenous maternal symbol for us."[17]

While the institution of Catholicism has been steadily railed against in the pursuit of racial, economic, and gender equalities, Catholic imagery and a relationship to the sacraments have maintained a privileged place in Mexican American identity.[18] On one level, in the tradition of Mexican American feminism, Mexican Catholic semiotics have provided a brown fertility goddess as a welcome respite from a secular world in which Santa Claus of the jolly capitalist belly, not the fecund womb of a poor, brown unwed mother, reigns over the nativity season. Santa (as opposed to the Virgin or the Magi) as the official logo of Christ's arrival is at odds with Catholic Mesoamerica and the anticapitalist spirituality of native, hemispheric Catholicism depicted in Castillo's prose.

Castillo mines the Catholic hagiographic genre that endeavors "enseñar deleitando" (to teach by entertaining). Her novel is full of advice and cautions for the edification and moral improvement of the reader. Sofia's campaign for mayor of Tome describes the process of converting a down-and-out village with a poor economic forecast into a socially conscious community with a sheep-grazing and wool-weaving cooperative modeled after another group that had saved its city from destitution. La Loca's favorite recipes are provided, as well as a host of doña Felicia's curatives, from sulfur for baldness to *limpias* (cleansings) used to undo bad intentions. With her amalgam of storytelling approaches, Castillo offers a new reading of Catholic traditions and Iberian hagiography that is life-affirming, inherently practical, Mesoamerican, and entirely feminist.

While Caridad's spiritual path embodies the recovery of past traditions for the community's regeneration, the dangerous character Francisco el Penitente personifies the most retrograde aspects of New Mexican Catholicism. As a New Mexican santero, Francisco represents the legacy of the Order of Penance and the fraternal religious institutions left over from New Mexico's colonial period. The dichotomy between Caridad and Francisco provides a vivid chiaroscuro of the spiritual frameworks available to Mexican Americans and to Nuevomexicanos, in particular.

Caridad's abilities are unlike the male-defined hierarchies of secular medical schools or Catholic clergy. Her metamorphosis transforms her from the Latina sexual body, categorized by the national border narrative as pathogen, to a source of woman-focused healing.

Moreover, the body is not to be regarded as the mere instrument of sin. The body itself houses wellness or sickness but, from the perspective of the curanderas, does not itself constitute a contaminant. The opposite is true for Francisco el Penitente. Rita Cano Alcalá notes that " Francisco, the Penitent, as his epithet suggests, adopts the most punitive elements of Catholic doctrine. He not only takes on the role of Jesus every year in the three-day Lenten procession—fasting, carrying the cross and wearing a crown of thorns—but he also takes frequent vows of silence and regularly practices self-flagellation and deprivation."[19] The role that Alcalá describes is a long-standing one in New Mexico, arriving with the Spanish colonizers toward the end of the sixteenth century.

Not only is Francisco el Penitente's legacy an echo of Catholicism's age of dread rather than compassion, it also reflects what was considered retrograde within the church itself during the colonial period. The first custodians of New Mexican religious art were the members of La Santa Hermandad de la Sangre de Nuestro Señor Jesucristo (Holy Brotherhood of the Blood of Our Lord Jesus Christ), who were more commonly known as the Penitentes (Penitents). In 1860, they changed their name to La Cofradía de Nuestro Padre Jesús Nazareno (Confraternity of Our Father Jesus of Nazareth) due to Bishop Lamy's objection to the flagellant connotations implied by the "Blood of Our Lord" in the prior title. The brotherhood insisted on public penance during Holy Week, which must have been an embarrassment to the bishop whose diocese would not conform to the Spanish crown's decision to outlaw public penance in 1777—nearly one hundred years earlier. New Mexico's isolation and distance from central Mexican viceregal authority allowed its residents to ignore the wishes of the court that felt that six hundred years of public flagellation had probably been enough. Aided by Father Antonio José Taos, who saw the attack on the Penitentes as an affront to New Mexican culture in general, this brotherhood was allowed to continue its rites and to adore, promote, and fashion regional devotional customs as it saw fit.

The Franciscan Order of Friars Minor and the Dominicans included among their ranks of confraternities the Third Order of the Penance. Active in New Mexico, the main contribution of the order to public life was the supervision of the annual Via Crucis (Way of the Cross) ceremony. The performance included a penitent representing Jesus on the day of crucifixion as he was made to carry the cross, bearing his burden along fourteen different stations. The Franciscan history of New Mexico is directly alluded to in Francisco el Penitente's name and vocation, but especially in his comportment. Each year he carries the cross during the Lenten procession and completes the role of Jesus by fasting and wearing a crown of thorns. His aunt Loretta resigns herself to never understanding the flagellant acts of her nephew:

> "I don't get it," Loretta sighed, shaking her head and walking out of the kitchen. Francisco el Penitente, or Franky as she had always called him, did not look up from his breakfast of blue corn atole and a side dish of huevos and posole. She was not objecting to the food, which she had prepared herself. It was good and what her husband, Franky's uncle, had had that morning. No, it was that Loretta caught Franky doing something real strange to his food that made her walk out.
>
> Well, face it, she said to herself, putting on her gardening gloves and going out to do some work on the vegetable garden,

> Franky always was kind of strange; but mixing up ashes from the fireplace into his food was a new one for the record. (191)

His desire to mortify the senses, as his aunt Loretta notices at the breakfast table, is one of the traits of Francisco's penitent lifestyle—and a benign form of self-punishment when compared to his attitude toward women.

His vocation of carving saint's images was that of "a simple man, often given to solitude, who worked alone. Sometimes a woman succumbed to the vocation, but his was rare" (96). His stint in Vietnam left him confused and embittered, and when his girlfriend left him, he lost interest in pursuing either women or studies. A classic misogynist, Francisco is capable of feeling admiration only for men. Instead of respect, what he is able to feel toward important women in his life is an idealization that lacks a realistic engagement with their multidimensionality. He loves his godmother (Caridad's teacher doña Felicia), but with a faraway regard that maintains her on a saintlike pedestal.

His final temptation will be that of his infatuation with Caridad, whom he cannot conceive apart from the virgin/whore dichotomy:

> And as Caridad became more and more fixed in his consciousness, worse than any of the pine splinters that stayed lodged in his palms, Francisco el Penitente became more determined to exorcise her out at whatever price to his body and soul. "More bitter than death I find the woman who is a hunter's trap, whose heart is a snare and whose hands are prison bonds," Francisco el Penitente recited. "He who is pleasing to God will escape her, but the sinner will be entrapped by her." (191)

In the end, his inability to deal with his own sexuality is what causes him to abduct Esmeralda, Caridad's sweetheart. When Esmeralda and Caridad are together again, they go to the Acoma Pueblo Indian Reservation to seek safety. Francisco follows them there. In an act of flight that constitutes both running away from the dangerous Francisco and running toward the call of Tsichtinako, Caridad and Esmeralda jump off the edge of the mesa, and Francisco hangs himself.

Francisco personifies elements of Catholicism left over from its medieval period: the mortification of the flesh, his attitude toward women, and his material expression of faith (seen in his physical inflictions and his creation of physical monuments) are all ways of putting forms and liturgies before charitable acts. Caridad, in name and action, represents the proactive virtues left over from colonial New Mexican religion and the community work of which devotional groups are capable. Charity instead of penitence: religious deeds of any denomination are useless unless they begin with sincere acts of giving.

So Far from God sees the valiant Sofia lose all four of her daughters in untimely and tragic deaths. La Loca perishes (the second time) from her inexplicable contraction of AIDS. Fe, unshakable believer in the American Dream, dies of cancer that she acquires while working with dangerous chemicals in the factory of a military subcontractor. Esperanza dies overseas as an investigative journalist, alluding to the disproportionate numbers of Chicanos and other minorities that die in foreign wars. Caridad is beckoned to serve Tsitchinako, and leaves the human domain in this deity's service. Instead of squandering her remaining years in misery, Sofia becomes the founder and charter member of M.O.M.A.S.: Mothers Of Saints And Martyrs.

An international association, this exclusive group symbolizes the restored empowerment of the womb as a sacred, regenerative site. Drawing another male/female binary, Castillo concludes her novel by comparing the medieval papacy to the group of bereaved yet triumphant mothers. Unlike the papal office that precluded the possibility of women members based on their supposed inferiority, the M.O.M.A.S. bear no hostility toward members of the opposite sex. The exclusion of men is based on the celebration of the womb, but not the castration of the male:

> But for a long time, a rumor followed las M.O.M.A.S. that the appointed board member Mothers were made to sit on chairs much like the ones that popes back in the beginning of their days were made to sit on after a woman who passed herself off as a man had been elected pope. In other words, a chair that was structured to prove that you were in fact a "mom" or, at least, could have been. What happened to that woman pope way back when, by the way, was that she was not only thrown off the throne for not being a man, but dragged through the streets and

> stoned to death. Nothing like that ever happened among the M.O.M.A.S.! ¡Hijo! Imagine las M.O.M.A.S. taking things that far to make sure that they all had wombs! (252)

Castillo's vision is not of a matriarchal society that reciprocates the violence perpetrated by patriarchy, but one that sustains the dream of social orderings that break this cycle of violence and imagines new ways to empower feminist, Mesoamerican epistemologies.

The Hummingbird's Daughter

On May 15, 1892, Mayo Indians crying "Viva la Santa de Cabora" attacked the regional center at Navojoa in Northern Mexico. Public officials and their supporters were shot down defending the town's main plaza, and blame for the assault was leveled at Teresa Urrea (1873–1906) (fig. 6.2). Just twenty-one years of age at the time of the attack, Teresa was hailed as a saint by many for her healing abilities and was remembered for the unwitting role she played as the "Mexican Joan of Arc." With *The Hummingbird's Daughter* (2005) Luis Alberto Urrea creates a historical novel about his family relation in which Mesoamerican ontology proves reliable, while Western constructions of being epitomize pathology: the Western actor can seldom be trusted to do more than swing from one self-serving desire to the next. Rather than imagining Teresita as a miraculously gifted anomaly, Urrea situates her abilities within the framework of a repertoire of Cahita Indian teachings. The indomitable Yaqui curandera Huila recognizes Teresita's power upon delivering her from her mother's womb, and keeps a watchful eye on Teresa's rmerging talents throughout her growing years. Through Huila, Urrea dispels the notion that Teresa's gifts came to her as an extracultural, purely supernatural transmission and instead emphasizes the rigors of her training and the earnest dialogue on matters spiritual and profane that she undertakes with Huila to demonstrate how healing was arbitrated by an ancient and autochthonous system of knowing.

Teresa was born the illegitimate child of Tomás Urrea, a powerful landowner, and Cayetana Chávez, the Tehueco Indian daughter of one of the ranch hands. The Tehuecos belonged to the Cahita group (along with the Yaquis and the Mayos), who cultivated the Fuerte

Figure 6.2 Teresa Urrea (Courtesy of Southwest Collection/Special Collections Library, Texas Tech University)

River Valley when the Spanish arrived.[20] Teresa was raised to adolescence by her mother's sister and spent most of her childhood in relative neglect—that is, unless her Aunt Tula was berating and battering her. Despite these inauspicious beginnings on the margins of Mexican ranch life, she mastered guitar, learned to read and write, and became a better rider than any of the seasoned ranch hands. Huila eventually takes Teresa under her tutelage. A revered figure who enjoyed relatively robust privileges at the top of the ranch workers' hierarchy, Huila performed as the physician to the Urrea clan and its workers, and moved the abused and neglected Teresita into her protection.

In her teen years, Tomás acknowledged Teresa as his daughter and began to educate her as a young woman of the *hacendado* class. Tomás's wife, Loreto Urrea, resided with their children in a nearby town. Soon after he moved Teresa into the Cabora manor with him, his young mistress, Gabriela, also joined the household. With Gabriela and Teresa as well as a thriving ranch and estate, Tomás finally matured into the role of patrón—ranch lord—and set aside the recklessness and womanizing that had characterized him.

The first page of the text conducts us into a universe in which the Cahita, referred to as "the People" throughout the novel, inhabit the center, whereas the Western world constitutes an intrusion from the periphery.

> On the big Santana rancho, the People had never seen paved streets, streetlamps, a trolley, or a ship. Steps were an innovation that seemed an occult work, stairways were the wicked cousins of ladders, and greatly to be avoided. Even the streets of Ocoroni, trod on certain Sundays when the People formed a long parade and left the safety of the hacienda to attend Mass, were dirt, or cobbled, not paved. The People thought all great cities had pigs in the streets and great muddy rivers of mule piss attracting hysterical swarms of wasps, and that all places were built of dirt and straw. They called little Cayetana the Hummingbird, using the mother tongue to say it: Semalú. (3)

In the above passage, Urrea does not provide a cultural backstory to render the scenario more intelligible to the Western reader. No explanation of demographics, ethnicity, linguistic groupings, or ecological characteristics is provided to bridge the distance between the Mesoamerican perspective and the West: the reader is to understand that the narrative domain belongs to the People. If this were a documentary, the camera would be in the hands of the People and aimed at the Yori (white person) to investigate their inexplicable occupations.

Just as the Mesoamerican civilizing project is granted greater currency in the text, so Teresita's healing is situated within the repertoire of Indian teachings. Shortly after the Urrea retinue is installed at the Cabora ranch, Huila takes her young charge to meet Manuelito, a Yaqui herbalist and *hechicero* (shaman), who initially refuses to train the young Teresa because her complexion is far too fair.

> "White," he said. "What little Indian blood you have will fall out when your first month begins."
>
> Teresita stamped her foot.
>
> "I am many things," she said. "But if you need to know, I have already bled, and I am still Indian!" (214)

As is the case when Huila provides instruction, Manuelito teaches Teresa the secrets of plants and herbs, letting her know which kinds of knowledge can be passed along to the Yori, and which teachings must be preserved among the People. Huila and Manuelito perform broad duties in their capacities as doctors, sages, and priests of the People, but they also are guardians of native epistemologies, taking care not to permit Yori ways to corrupt their ways of knowing.

Teresa's maternal inheritance is inseparable from her Indian patrimony; Cayetana Chávez, "La Semalú"—"the Hummingbird"—is the embodiment of the People. The mother's significance is most apparent in the novel's matrilineal title but also is in the recurring symbol of the hummingbird, which outweighs the Semalú's personal appearance in the extraordinary life of her daughter. Readers alert to the problems of Mexican and Mexican American identity in arts and letters will appreciate Urrea's elegant reversal of the "myth of *la chingada*" (myth of the "fucked one") of Octavio Paz's *Labyrinth of Solitude* that is mentioned briefly in chapter 4. By empowering Teresa's mother and ennobling her activity, even when this is as ephemeral and fleeting as a flutter of hummingbird wings around Teresa's body or the Semalú's stealthy exit from her daughter's life in the dark of night, Urrea counters the notion of Mexican identity crisis—based on the shame of the conquistador's violent pairing with the humiliated native woman—by envisioning the native mother as powerful and transcendent, and one whose precarious condition is to be revered rather than derided. La Semalú is not the "fucked one." She is neither a traitor to be reviled nor a victim whose abduction is to be referred to in the muted tones reserved for the lamentable, but a heroine whose story is life-giving and nation building.

> Cayetana greeted that dawn with a concoction made with coffee beans and burned corn kernels. As the light poured out of the eastern sea and splashed into windows from coast to coast, Mexicans rose and went to their million kitchens and cooking fires to pour their first rations of coffee. A tidal wave of coffee rushed west across the land. . . . The heavy-eyed stared into the round mirrors of their cups and regarded their own dark reflections. And Cayetana Chávez, too, lifted a cup, her coffee reboiled from yesterday's grounds and grits, sweet with spoons of sugarcane

> syrup, and lightened by thin blue milk stolen with a few quick squeezes from one of the patrón's cows.
>
> So what were they? Every Mexican was a diluted Indian, invaded by milk like the coffee in Cayetana's cup. Afraid, after the Conquest and the Inquisition, of their own brown wrappers, they colored their faces with powder, covered their skins in perfumes and European silks and American habits. Yet for all their beaver hats and their lace veils, the fine citizens of the great cities knew they had nothing that would ever match the ancient feathers of the quetzal . . . (9)

Here, we find that the notions of Cayetana's cup and the national womb are co-identified. La Semalú is the hummingbird, the Mesoamerican Holy Spirit whose pregnant body houses the past centuries and the present hour. Internalized colonization in this passage is overcome by the clamor of the ancients. The quetzal feather comes from the mystical bird-serpent that was venerated as Quetzalcoatl, one of the earliest deities of the Americas. The West cannot hope to compete with the quetzal's feathers, and the hummingbird becomes a million Mexicans, a million quetzal feathers, whose dark reflection can never be sullied by the colonizer's misuse of native women; whose worth is not contingent on the fickle tides of European fashions.

By privileging the maternal relationship between Teresita and her Indian mother, Urrea reclaims the oppressed dark-skinned mother that is so frequently demeaned in the optic of the Mexican nation. In Urrea's prose, the Western mind that dismisses the Mesoamerican project is the mirage—a shadow disturbance cast by the fever mind, and the author sorts through the subterfuge in order to cure. In an interview appended to the paperback edition, he plainly describes the preference for Western derived identities and curatives over Mesoamerican ones as illness: "The more I entered the shamanic world, the less I wanted to write about it. I confessed this once to Native American author Linda Hogan. I told her my 'Western mind' couldn't wrap itself around all this mystical stuff. She said, 'Honey, the Western mind is a fever. It will pass.'"[21]

What is this Western mind? According to the above quote, the disdain for "mystical stuff" is an illness that subsides with patience and time—and the determined cultivation of its alternative. If Western mind is an illness, it can pass. If Western mind is a fever, then it can be cured.

Honoring the discredited, nonlinear, affective world of native medicine, Urrea restores the "discredited knowledge" that Gay Wilentz describes in *Healing Narratives: Women Writers Curing Cultural Dis-ease* (2000): "For people from oppressed cultures, this means reclaiming personal wellness through self-esteem and the "discredited" knowledge (to quote Toni Morrison) of a culture's healing practices."[22] Decolonial thinking teaches us that our disdain for the epistemologies offered by indigenous intellectual traditions is, in the words of Fernández Retamar, "but another proof of our subjection to the colonialist perspective of history that has been imposed on us, causing names, dates, circumstances and truths to vanish from our consciousness."[23]

While privileging native truths throughout, the text does not resort to the categorical demonization of "Whitey." The first time *Hummingbird* reveals a perspective that comes from a Yori, it is through the eyes of Don Tomás. The fair-colored offspring of privileged landowners, Don Tomás is content in his world in which the steady flow of luxuries and deferential subjects that cross his path are regarded as nothing less than a birthright. The material world before him is narrated sumptuously to show how the young Don Tomás's palate lingers on the seductive perfume of food and women alike.

> With liquid on the mind, it was not long before they found the notorious El Farolito cantina. There, they ate raw shellfish still gasping under tides of lime juice and hot sauce with great crystals of salt that cracked between the teeth of the men. Naked women writhed to a tuba-and-drum combo. The men regarded this display with joy, though Aguirre made the effort to feel guilty about it. (6)

Here is a man thoroughly at home in the world of ostentation. Impervious to any form of religious dedication, he leaves the spiritual life to his wife, Loretto, to whom he devotes polite overtures of conjugal acquaintance for the sake of leaving heirs, without committing the impropriety of regarding her with any real passion. This heathen Yori and his advanced condition of megalomania—pandemic, it would seem, among the Yoris—are humanized in the text when he is cured of his pathological egotism and learns to sympathize with the plight of the People.

The subversion of Tomás's Yori identity, and his gradual identification with his daughter and the downtrodden people who receive her ministrations, evolves throughout the course of the story. Our first introduction to Tomás's affection for the natives is revealed by Cayetana's pregnancy. The insemination of the ranch women by the boss is a pan-American phenomenon known on Mexican haciendas and on Anglo plantations alike. Almost a rite of passage in colonizer/colonized relations, in places like Brazil, cases were recalled in which it was impossible for the young white aristocrat to achieve arousal with his white wife without smelling the clothing of the slave girls that he visited. His constant hunger for Indian virgins does little to ennoble the figure of Tomás Urrea in *Hummingbird,* and much less his strict policy of using them in their early teen years and using them only once—lest they presume familiarity. Additionally, Tomás has no interest in knowing whether the lighter-skinned births amongst his workers are attributable to his own appetites. This first impression of a young prince delighting in his rutting privileges is not an especially endearing one.

However, a deeper sense of caring is soon conveyed when, on a whim, Tomás enjoins his head housekeeper, Huila, to sit down to supper with him. As she makes her way noisily through her meal, she asks him to explain his fondness for the People.

> "And you," she said, "what do you care if an old ranchero lives or dies? Why do you like the People so much? Aside from the girls. Everybody knows why you like the girls."
>
> He cleared his throat. This girl business was best unanswered. But the rest of it. At last! Something to talk about!
>
> "The People!" he said.
>
> "That's what I said. Are you deaf?"
>
> "Don Refugio," he finally replied. (42)

Tomás confides in Huila the unorthodox relationship he had shared with Don Refugio, an Indian ranch hand who had survived a massacre as violent and heartless as any depicted in the pages of America's colonization. Here we discover the inversion of the Indian–Yori relationship that was key to Tomás's formation. Instead of the Indian being humanized by gaining proximity to the white man, we have the young man becoming humanized and gaining a perspective of compassion and fellowship with other beings through his close relationship with Don Refugio.

The tale of Don Refugio prefigures Tomás's conclusive transformation, which takes place when he finally comes to terms with his daughter's unexplainable vocation. Throughout the narrative, he has either scoffed at or stormed against her ministrations, until one quiet night when both father and daughter are both independently drawn to the kitchen when they could not sleep. They hear a soft tapping on the back door—when Tomás opens it, he is blasted with the smell of rotten garbage and sickness. It is an Indian boy with bare, blackened feet, toenails split and bloody, with ruined pants and no shirt, and his hair coming off his scalp in stiff spikes. The child's parents are dead. Who took care of him? Dogs. Don Tomás is repelled by the child's condition and scolds him for daring to disturb the family home, but Teresita immediately welcomes the boy and makes him comfortable.

> He went to the chair. Teresita had snipped away most of the boy's hair, leaving gooey bristles among which the sluggish lice could be seen.
>
> "Pluck," she told her father.
>
> "Pluck what?"
>
> "Lice."
>
> "You're kidding."
>
> "No, I'm not kidding. Pluck them and pop them."
>
> "But I'll get pus on my fingers!"
>
> "You can wash your hands."
>
> "But it's disgusting!"
>
> "No, Father. Letting an orphan suffer is disgusting."
>
> "Chingado," he said.
>
> He gingerly pinched one of the awful little beasts and popped it between his nails. It was oddly satisfying.
>
> "Got the bastard," he noted.
>
> "Good work."
>
> . . . They plucked lice for so long that the boy fell asleep under their fingers. Tomás wiped so much pus on the front of his pants that they had two ugly stains. For the first time in his life, he felt—well, saintly. (403)

Prior to this experience, Teresa's father had never seen lice, although this experience helped him discover that everyone outside of the big house suffered from them. Teresa is surprised to discover that he has such little knowledge of the lives of the People right outside his door: "She looked up at him and wondered what it felt like to be so ignorant of the world (401)." The next day, Gabrisela finds the three of them asleep together on the couch, an image that shows he has dispelled Yori ignorance and turned toward Mesoamerican truth. This was achieved by means of his daughter's centrifugal transmission of healing.

Obviously, as a miracle worker, Teresa could not remain anonymous for long. Enormous crowds come to the Urrea ranch in Cabora, and some of these are hostile to the government of Porfirio Díaz. Despite her father's urgings, she refuses no pilgrim, nor does she disrupt her ministrations in any way. Angering and alarming both church and state, Teresa and Tomás are finally detained and tortured before they are expelled from the Mexican Republic. The novel concludes with her and her father facing exile and traveling to the United States. Her life concludes some fourteen years later in Clifton, Arizona, in 1906.

In William Curry Holden's fictional treatment of Teresa Urrea published in 1978, he narrates the disgust of Don Lauro, a revolutionary activist and close family friend of the Urreas, upon their eviction from Mexico. "Don Lauro could not resist a parting thrust. 'I wonder,' he said, 'what will happen to a government that expels its nation's most gifted and Christian-like woman.'"[24] *The Hummingbird's Daughter* ends with Mexico sending Teresa away to the United States, a scene depicted as a woeful loss to the Mexican nation. Rather than a pollutant flowing into the imagined purity of the Anglo national bloodstream, we have the scenario of Mexico's spirit being drained as it loses its gifted children forever to the great, dark North.

Conclusion

In the United States, the pathogen myth naturalizes the disenfranchisement of its Mesoamerican population, particularly imprinting Latina womanhood with the stigma of pollution. In three contemporary novels by prominent Chicano and Chicana writers, woman healers contest the dominant culture's construal of Mesoamerican women as pathogens. Anaya's Ultima emphasizes ecological knowledge as an animistic, indigenous foundation of wisdom. Corresponding with the early Chicano movement's aims, *Bless Me, Ultima* revisions the role that the Catholic Church plays in developing a practical strategy for mestizos to cope with suffering and the subtleties of moral integrity. The radical women-of-color feminism in Castillo's writing advocates gender equality alongside cultural diversity, rejecting the ethnic essentialism of the early movement when this came at the expense of women's emancipation. Finally, Urrea articulates a hemispheric construction of Teresita's medical authority. Each of these solutions belongs to a unique moment in the Mesoamerican struggle for self-representation and self-determination, but all seek to restore devalued knowledge transmitted by women who propose a cure for the fever of the Western mind.

7

To Anahuac

"I PRAY FOR YOUR BOOK THE WAY I PRAY FOR MY PEOPLE." When Agustina Martínez told me these words on my visit to Huautla de Jiménez about a year after I had submitted my doctoral dissertation in 2003, I was humbled by a sense of duty, and more than a little guilt. While I had always intended to pursue publication, I had spent the year following my graduation working on my prose writing and preparing for my new life as an assistant professor. Although these are not unworthy pursuits, I was reminded that by conducting research in the area of Mesoamerican peoples, more is at stake than an ISBN number and a credit on the curriculum vitae—I was burdened with a community cargo. The privilege of study conferred on me by a host of outside individuals and circumstances (please see the acknowledgments at the beginning of this volume for a woefully abbreviated account) is not a route away from my Mesoamerican communities, but rather the pathway I needed to travel to help combat colonial irrationality, restore memory, and envision and implement new solutions.

I take no pleasure in the parallelism between this study's introduction and its conclusion. Beginning in California, where I sought Mesoamerican models of intellectual agency during the time of Proposition 187 and Proposition 209, by which California voters passed legislation restricting access to hospitals and schools for undocumented Californians and eliminated affirmative action in public institutions, respectively, I type the conclusion from my kitchen in Chicago's largely Mexican Pilsen neighborhood, in a country where reason again is hostage to the fever of the Western mind. Two months ago, Arizona Governor Jan Biewer signed Senate Bill 1070, a discriminatory law that essentially legalizes racial profiling to facilitate the prosecution and deportation of undocumented residents. Ethnic studies are increasingly demonized in schools around the nation, where budget constraints become the pretext to ensure the naturalization of elite discourse and historical amnesia, while the increasingly militarized border and the mainstream reporting on narco-violence encourage the metaphors of Latinos as invaders, parasites, burdens, and contaminants. As in the mid-'90s, feelings of humiliation and anger form a part of the book that is now in your hands.

The need to protect and promote our knowledge—our medicine—is greater than ever before. I have tried to make this case by using the theoretical tools offered by the fields of social epistemology, feminist historical analysis, performance studies, and literary criticism. Criticism, José Martí has noted, means the application of criteria. What are the criteria—the values and judgments—applied by the referees of official intellectual competency? As a denizen of the West, my entire formal education had equipped me to regard secular philosophical work as the most exalted of humanistic pursuits, because I had been taught, both at home and in school, that critical-empirical work loomed far above the "primitive" arts of healing and shamanizing. Upon interrogating the civilizing project of the West, we discern how theories of knowledge conspire to sediment political hierarchies, and to dismiss or trivialize the core values of Mesoamerican intellectual work. It would not be in the Western realm of dueling discourses where I finally located native women's knowledge transmissions, but in the centrifugal plane that bore no resemblance to this battlefield.

"To Anahuac." My final chapter's title represents a dedication as much as it does a destination: *To Anahuac, with love/To Anahuac, or bust*. To plot Anahuac on a map and say that it denotes a specific location would be to weigh it and measure it and watch it get sold off, piece by piece. Within moments of leaving Chicago, I am surrounded by the cornfields that are yet another vestige of Anahuac's expanse. *To Anahuac, with love/To Anahuac, or bust.*

My research has helped introduce me to Mesoamerican ways of knowing, and it is offered here with the hope that others who have been distanced from hemispheric traditions are inspired to find new ways to diagnose the consequences of the capitalist and colonial disease load that is our privilege and responsibility to cure.

Punto.

Notes

Chapter 1

1. Ana Castillo, *Massacre of the Dreamers: Essays on Xicanisma*. New York: Plume Books, 1994.

2. See Robin May Schott, *Discovering Feminist Philosophy: Knowledge, Ethics, Politics* (Lanham, MD: Rowman and Littlefield, 2003), 57.

3. I will use the spelling *Chicana,* rather than *Xicana,* in the rest of this introduction. I enjoy the continuity signified in the rephrasing of *Mexica* through time: Mexica→Mexico→Mexican→Xicana, as well as the revisioning of *Chicano* and its historical cargo that was energetically undertaken by Ana Castillo and many other Chicana thinkers and writers in the 1990s. As with other communities dealing with the fragmentation of colonization and diaspora, particular names, spellings, and testimonies of Mesoamerican and mestizo peoples resist sedimentation.

4. Michèle Le Dœuff, *Hipparchia's Choice: An Essay Concerning Women, Philosophy, etc.,* trans. Trista Selous (Oxford: Blackwell, 1991).

5. Castillo, *Massacre of the Dreamers,* 8–9.

6. Miguel León-Portilla, *Aztec Thought and Culture: A Study of the Ancient Nahuatl Mind,* trans. Jack Emory Davis (Norman: University of Oklahoma Press, 1963), 3.

7. Abram, David. *The Spell of the Sensuous: Perception and Language in a More-than-Human World* (New York: Vintage Books, 1997).

Chapter 2

1. David Carrasco, *Religions of Mesoamerica: Cosmovision and Ceremonial Centers* (San Francisco: Harper Collins, 1990).

2. Bernardino de Sahagún, *Florentine Codex,* trans. Arthur J. O. Anderson and Charles E. Dibble (Salt Lake City: University of Utah Press, 1953), 10:14.

3. Alfredo Lopez Austin, *The Myths of the Opossum: Pathways of Mesoamerican Mythology,* trans. Thelma Ortiz de Montellano and Bernard Ortiz de Montellano (Albuquerque: University of New Mexico Press, 1993).

4. Hernando Ruíz de Alarcón, *Aztec Sorcerers in Seventeenth Century Mexico: The Treatise on Superstitions by Hernando Ruiz de Alarcón,* trans. Michael Coe and Gordon Whittaker (Albany: Institute for Mesoamerican Studies, State University of New York at Albany, 1982), 220.

5. Marvin Harris, *Our Kind: Who We Are, Where We Came From, Where We Are Going* (New York: Harper Perennial, 1989), 324–30.

6. Diego Durán, *The History of the Indies of New Spain,* trans. Doris Heyden (Norman: University of Oklahoma Press, 1994), 35.

7. Ibid., 44.

8. Alfredo López Austin, *The Human Body and Ideology: Concepts of the Ancient Nahuas,* trans. Thelma Ortiz de Montellano and Bernard Ortiz de Montellano (Salt Lake City: University of Utah Press, 1988), 54–55.

9. Ibid., 89–159.

10. See Thomas Buckley and Alma Gottlieb, eds. *Blood Magic: The Anthropology of Menstruation* (Berkeley: University of California Press, 1988); Marvin Harris, *Cannibals and Kings: Origins of Cultures* (New York: Vintage Books, 1977); and Inga Clendinnen, *Aztecs: An Interpretation* (Cambridge: Cambridge University Press, 1991).

11. Buckley and Gottlieb, *Blood Magic,* 6.

12. López Austin, *Human Body,* 179.

13. Clendinnen, *Aztecs,* 158.

14. Sahagún, *Florentine Codex,* 2:21, 48.

15. Durán, Diego. *Book of the Gods and Rites and the Ancient Calendar,* trans. Fernando Horcasitas and Doris Heyden (Norman: University of Oklahoma Press, 1971), 424.

16. Ibid., 222.

17. Ibid., 428.

18. Sahagún, *Florentine Codex,* 2:23.

19. Cecelia Klein, ed. *Gender in Pre-Hispanic Mesoamerica* (Washington, DC: Dumbarton Oaks Research Library Collection, 2001), 110.

20. Miguel León-Portilla, *Aztec Thought and Culture: A Study of the Ancient Nahuatl Mind,* trans. Jack Emory Davis (Norman: University of Oklahoma Press, 1963), 45–48.

21. Elizabeth M. Brumfiel, "Asking about Aztec Gender," *Gender in Pre-Hispanic Mesoamerica,* ed. Cecelia F. Klein (Washington, DC: Dumbarton Oaks Research Library Collection), 63.

22. Sahagún, *Florentine Codex,* 2:21, 54.

23. Ibid., 7:10, 27.

24. The vicious crossroads haunters have survived the centuries as well as Spanish rule and entered the global age in the form of La Llorona, the "Weeping Woman" of Mexican children's stories. Recast in modern fable, she is typically a

vindictive woman who has drowned her own children to avenge her husband's neglect and abuse, and her repentant soul haunts the night in anguish and rage as she seeks her lost children. She sometimes curses, drowns, or confounds the children and adults she meets, but most pointedly her wrath and dread are aimed for the hearts and minds of the very young, who are the most vulnerable to her thrall. The Cihuateteo were Cihuacóatl's agents, often depicted with her skeletal face, stalking children in the darkness in a merciless mourning.

25. Sahagún, *Florentine Codex,* 6:26, 149.

26. Ibid., 6:27, 155.

27. Raymond A. Bucko, *The Lakota Ritual of the Sweat Lodge: History and Contemporary Practice* (Lincoln: University of Nebraska Press, 1998), 203.

28. Hernando Ruíz de Alarcón, *Aztec Sorcerers in Seventeenth Century Mexico: The Treatise on Superstitions by Hernando Ruiz de Alarcón,* trans. Michael D. Coe and Gordon Whittaker (Albany: Institute for Mesoamerican Studies, State University of New York, 1982), 220.

29. Ibid., 30.

30. Sahagún, *Florentine Codex,* 6:29, 161.

31. Ibid., 162.

32. Durán, *History.*

Chapter 3

1. Asunción Lavrin, ed., *Latin American Women: Historical Perspectives* (Westport, CT: Greenwood Press, 1978).

2. Jean Dangler, *Mediating Fictions: Women Healers and the Go-Between in Medieval and Early Modern Iberia* (Cranbury, NJ: Bucknell University Press, 2001), 36.

3. Ibid., 43.

4. Roberto Moreno de los Arcos, "New Spain's Inquisition for Indians from the Sixteenth to the Nineteenth Century," in *Cultural Encounters,* ed. Mary Elizabeth Perry and Anne J. Cruz (Berkeley: University of California Press, 1991), 23–36.

5. Mary E. Giles, *Women in the Inquisition: Spain and the New World* (Baltimore: Johns Hopkins University Press, 1999), 78.

6. Geraldine McKendrick and Angus MacKay, "Visionaries and Affective Spirituality during the First Half of the Sixteenth Century," in *Cultural Encounters: The Impact of the Inquisition in Spain and the New World,* ed. Mary Elizabeth Perry and Anne J. Cruz (Berkeley: University of California Press, 1991), 93–101.

7. Ibid., 99.

8. Josefina Muriel, *Cultura femenina novohispana* (Mexico City: Universidad Nacional Autónoma de México, 1982), 315. See also Elisa Sampson Vera Tudela, *Colonial Angels: Narratives of Gender and Spirituality in Mexico, 1580–1750* (Austin: University of Texas Press, 2000).

9. Muriel, *Cultura femenina novohispana,* 321.

10. Elisa Sampson Vera Tudela. *Colonial Angels: Narratives of Gender and Spirituality in Mexico, 1580–1750* (Austin: University of Texas Press, 2000), 37–38.

11. Ibid., 39.

12. Jacqueline Holler, "More Sins than the Queen of England: Marina de San Miguel before the Mexican Inquisition," in *Women in the Inquisition: Spain and the New World,* ed. Mary E. Giles (Baltimore: Johns Hopkins University Press, 1999), 217.

13. Ibid., 223.

14. Ibid., 227–28.

15. Arenal, Electa, and Amanda Powell, eds., *The Answer/La Respuesta,* by Sor Juana Ines de la Cruz (New York: Feminist Press, 1994), 169.

16. Octavio Castro López, *Sor Juana y el "Primero sueño"* (Xalapa, Veracruz: Universidad Veracruzana, 1982).

17. Alan S. Trueblood, *A Sor Juana Anthology* (Cambridge: Harvard University Press, 1988), 360.

18. Octavio Paz, *Sor Juana Inés de la Cruz o las Trampas de la Fe* (Mexico City, México: Editorial Seix Barral, 1982), 361.

19. Ibid., 367.

20. Georgina Sabat-Rivers, "A Feminist Rereading of Sor Juana's *Dream,*" in *Feminist Perspectives on Sor Juana Inés de la Cruz,* ed. Stephanie Merrim (Detroit: Wayne State University Press, 1999), 157.

21. Karen Viera Powers, *Women in the Crucible of the Conquest: The Gendered Genesis of Spanish American Society, 1500–1600* (Albuquerque: University of New Mexico Press, 2005).

22. Julia Tuñón Pablos, *Women in Mexico: A Past Unveiled,* trans. Alan Hynds (Austin: University of Texas Press, 1999).

23. Anna Macías, *Against All Odds: The Feminist Movement in Mexico to 1940* (Westport, CT: Greenwood Press, 1982), 7–9.

24. Shirlene Soto, *Emergence of the Modern Mexican Woman: Her Participation in Revolution and the Struggle for Equality* (Denver: Arden, 1990), 11–12.

25. Josefina Muriel, *Los recogimientos de mujeres: Respuesta a una problemática social novohispana* (Mexico City: Universidad Nacional Autónoma de México, 1974), 226.

26. Macías, *Against All Odds,* 32–35.

27. E. V. Niemeyer Jr. *Revolution at Querétaro: The Mexican Constitutional Convention of 1916–1917* (Austin: University of Texas Press, 1974), 86.

28. Ibid., 90.

29. Soto, *Emergence of the Modern Mexican Woman,* 63.

30. Ibid., 116.

31. Ibid., 115.

32. Jocelyn Olcott, *Revolutionary Women in Postrevolutionary Mexico* (Durham: Duke University Press, 2005), 43.

33. Ibid., 103.

34. Ibid., 46–47.

35. Stewart Voss, "Nationalizing the Revolution: Culmination and Circumstance," in *Provinces of the Revolution: Essays on Regional Mexican History, 1910–1929*, ed. Thomas Benjamin and Mark Wasserman (Albuquerque: University of New Mexico Press, 1990), 296–99.

36. Olcott, *Revolutionary Women in Postrevolutionary Mexico*, 233.

Chapter 4

1. Roberta Avery, "Surviving—and Thriving" *thestar.com* March 12, 2009, http://www.thestar.com/article/272307.

2. David Abram, *The Spell of the Sensuous: Perception and Language in a More-than-Human World* (New York: Vintage Books, 1996).

3. Frank L. Lipp, "A Comparative Analysis of Southern Mexican and Guatemalan Shamans," in *Mesoamerican Healers*, ed. Brad H. Huber and Alan R. Sandstrom (Austin: University of Texas Press, 2001), 95–116.

4. Eliseo Torres, *Healing with Herbs and Rituals* (Albuquerque: University of New Mexico Press, 2006).

5. Noemi Quesada, "The Inquisition's Repression of Curanderos," in *Cultural Encounters*, ed. Mary Elizabeth Perry and Anne J. Cruz (Berkeley: University of California Press, 1991).

6. See Jacqueline Holler, "More Sins than the Queen of England: Marina de San Miguel before the Mexican Inquisition," and Richard E. Greenleaf, "Historiography of the Mexican Inquisition," both in *Cultural Encounters: The Impact of the Inquisition in Spain and the New World*, ed. Mary Elizabeth Perry and Anne J. Cruz (Berkeley: University of California Press, 1991).

7. J. Jorge Klor de Alva, "Colonizing Souls: The Failure of the Indian Inquisition and the Rise of Penitential Discipline," in *Cultural Encounters: The Impact of the Inquisition in Spain and the New World*, ed. Mary Elizabeth Perry and Anne J. Cruz (Berkeley: University of California Press, 1991).

8. Sheila Cosminsky, "Maya Midwives of Southern Mexico and Guatemala," in *Mesoamerican Healers*, ed. Brad H. Huber and Alan R. Sandstrom (Austin: University of Texas Press, 2001), 179–210.

9. William M. Denevan, *The Native Population in the Americas in 1492* (Madison: University of Wisconsin Press, 1992), 7.

10. Henry F. Dobyns, *Their Number Become Thinned: Native American Population Dynamics in Eastern North America* (Knoxville: University of Tennessee Press, 1983).

11. Luz María Hernández Sáenz and George M. Foster, "Curers and Their Cures in Colonial New Spain and Guatemala: The Spanish Component," in *Mesoamerican Healers*, ed. Brad H. Huber and Alan R. Sandstrom (Austin: University of Texas Press, 2001), 22.

12. Ibid., 31.

13. Ibid., 19–46.

14. Roland H. Bainton, *Hunted Heretic: The Life and Death of Michael Servetus, 1511–1553,* new ed. (Providence: Blackstone Editions, [1953] 2005).

15. Carlos Viesca Treviño, "*Curanderismo* in Mexico and Guatemala: Its Historical Evolution from the Sixteenth to the Nineteenth Century," in *Mesoamerican Healers,* ed. Brad H. Huber and Alan R. Sandstrom (Austin: University of Texas Press, 2001), 33.

16. Walter D. Mignolo, *Coloniality, Subaltern Knowledges, and Border Thinking: Local Theories/Global Designs* (Princeton: Princeton University Press, 2000).

17. William R. Holland, *Medicina maya en los altos de Chiapas,* trans. Daniel Cazes (Mexico, DF: Instituto Nacional Indigenista, 1963), 232–33.

18. Brad H. Huber and Alan R. Sandstrom, eds. *Mesoamerican Healers* (Austin: University of Texas Press, 2001).

19. Jaime Tomás Page Pliego, *El mandato de los dioses: Medicina entre los Tzotziles de Chamula y Chenalhó, Chiapas* (Mexico City: Universidad Nacional Autónoma de México, 2005), 83–89.

20. Ibid., 88.

21. Unless otherwise noted, all translations in this chapter are my own.

22. Viesca Treviño, *Ticiotl: Conceptos médicos de los antiguos mexicanos* (Mexico City: Universidad Nacional Autónoma de México, 1997), 26–27.

23. Ibid., 19–46.

24. Samuel Karchmer Krivitsky, "La ginecología y la obstétrica," in *Contribuciones mexicanos al conocimiento medico,* ed. Hugo Aréchega and Juan Somolinos Palencia (Mexico City: Fondo de Cultura Económica, 1993), 281.

25. Hernández Sáenz and Foster, "Curers and Their Cures," 38.

26. Ibid., 39.

27. Sheila Cosminsky, "Maya Midwives of Southern Mexico and Guatemala," in *Mesoamerican Healers,* ed. Brad H. Huber and Alan R. Sandstrom (Austin: University of Texas Press, 2001), 179–210.

28. Rosita Arvigo and Nadine Epstein, *Sastun: One Woman's Apprenticeship with a Maya Healer and Their Efforts to Save the Vanishing Tradition of Rainforest Medicine* (San Francisco: Harper, 1995).

29. Page Pliego, *El mandato de los dioses,* 20.

30. Leanne M. Fecteau, "The Ayahuasca Patent Revocation: Raising Questions about Current US Patent Policy," http://www.bc.edu/bc_org/avp/law/lwsch/journals/bctwj/21_1/03_FMS.htm.

31. Carole Browner, "The Management of Reproduction in an Egalitarian Society," in *Women as Healers: Cross-Cultural Perspectives,* ed. Carol McClain (London: Rutgers University Press, 1989), 58–71.

32. James W. Dow, "Central and North Mexican Shamans," in *Mesoamerican Healers,* ed. Brad H. Huber and Alan R. Sandstrom (Austin: University of Texas Press, 2001), 92.

33. Virginia Mellado Campos, Armando Sánchez Reyes, Paolo Femia, Alfredo Navarro Magdaleno, Erique Erosa Solana, Daisy Mary Bonilla Contreras, and

Marina del Socorro Domínguez Hernández, *La Medicina tradicional de los pueblos indígenas de México* (Mexico City: Instituto Nacional Indigenista, 1994), 277.

34. Cosminsky, "Maya Midwives of Southern Mexico and Guatemala," 186.

35. Ibid., 187.

36. Viesca Treviño, "*Curanderismo* in Mexico and Guatemala," 48.

37. Holland, *Medicina maya en los altos de Chiapas,* 174–80.

38. James Clay Young, *Medical Choice in a Mexican Village* (New Brunswick: Rutgers University Press, 1981).

Chapter 5

1. Norma Alarcón, "Chicana Feminism: In the Tracks of 'The' Native Woman," in *Living Chicana Theory,* ed. Carla Trujillo (Berkeley: Third Woman, 1998).

2. Frantz Fanon, *The Wretched of the Earth,* trans. Constance Farrington (New York: Grove Press, 1963), 224.

3. Ibid., 227.

4. Gloria Anzaldúa, *Borderlands/La frontera: The New Mestiza* (San Francisco: Aunt Lute Books, 1987), 21.

5. Jane H. Hill, "Women's Speech in Modern Mexicano," in *Language, Gender, and Sex in Comparative Perspective,* ed. Susan U. Philips, Susan Steele, and Christine Tanz (Cambridge: Cambridge University Press, 1987), 121.

6. Ibid., 159.

7. Saskia Sassen, *Globalization and Its Discontents* (New York: New Press, 1998), 84.

8. Eckart Boege, *Los mazatecos ante la nación* (Mexico City: Siglo Veintiuno Editores, 1988), 121.

9. James C. Scott, *Domination and the Arts of Resistance: Hidden Transcripts* (New Haven: Yale University Press, 1990), 80.

10. *Velada* is the Spanish translation of the Mazatec *vi yo choan* ("stay awake").

11. Álvaro Estrada, *María Sabina: Her Life and Chants*, trans. Henry Munn (Santa Barbara: Ross-Erikson, 1981), 132.

12. Ibid., 213.

13. Wasson was not the first outsider to partake in the ritual, just the first one to work with Sabina and widely disseminate his own views on the matter.

14. Estrada, *María Sabina,* 91.

15. Ibid., 20.

16. Ibid., 211.

17. Friedrich Nietzsche, *Beyond Good and Evil,* trans. Helen Zimmern (Buffalo, NY: Prometheus, 1989), 56.

18. Nestor García Canclini, *Transforming Modernity: Popular Culture in Mexico,* trans. Lidia Lozano (Austin: University of Texas Press, 1993), 45.

19. Preface by Rothenberg in Estrada, *María Sabina,* 8.

20. John Tomlinson, *Globalization and Culture* (Chicago: University of Chicago Press, 1999), 84.

21. Boege, *Los mazatecos ante la nación,* 26 (my translation).

22. Ibid., 50.

23. Guillermo Gómez-Peña, *Dangerous Border Crossers* (New York: Routledge, 2000), 101.

24. Ibid., 105.

Chapter 6

1. Maria V. Ruíz, "Border Narratives, HIV/AIDS, and Latina/o Health in the United States: A Cultural Analysis," *Feminist Media Studies* 2, no. 1 (2002), 37–62.

2. Ibid., 41.

3. Ricardo Cruz, "Católicos por la Raza Papers." California Ethnic and Multicultural Archives, University of California at Santa Barbara, Box 15, Folder 6.

4. Ibid.

5. Ibid.

6. See Carlos G. Vélez-Ibáñez, "Carlos G. Vélez-Ibáñez Sterilization Papers ca. 1972–1979," Chicano Studies Research Center Library, University of California at Los Angeles; and Vicki L. Ruiz, *From out of the Shadows: Mexican Women in Twentieth-Century America,* 10th anniv. ed. (New York: Oxford University Press, 2008).

7. Rudolfo Acuña, *Occupied America: A History of Chicanos,* 3rd ed.(New York: Harper and Row, 1988), 279–81.

8. Ibid., 266–69.

9. See Marta Cotera, "Feminism: The Chicana and Anglo Versions: A Historical Analysis," in *Twice a Minority: Mexican American Women,* ed. Margarita B. Melville (St. Louis: Mosby, 1980), 217–34.

10. Ruiz, *From out of the Shadows,* 108.

11. "Gabacho" is the Chicano movement's synonym for its predecessor "gringo."

12. Alicia Gaspar de Alba, "There's No Place like Aztlán: Embodied Aesthetics in Chicana Art," *New Centennial Review* 4, no. 2 (2004): 103–40.

13. Luís Leal, "Chicano Literary History: Origin and Development," Julian Samora Research Institute Occasional Paper 8 (1996). East Lansing: Michigan State University, http://www.jsri.msu.edu/RandS/research/ops/oc08.html. Leal states,

> After reading these early works, I reached the conclusion that the history of Chicano literature should include everything written before 1848 (published and in manuscript form) as it rightfully forms part of the Chicano cultural inheritance. As far as we know, no people has rejected its literary inheritance.

> The history of American literature does not begin in 1776; it includes all works in existence since the arrival of the Pilgrims in the seventeenth century. The literary history of Mexico does not begin in 1821; nor do we say that Sor Juana's poetry belongs to the history of Spanish literature (5).

14. David Abram, *The Spell of the Sensuous: Perception and Language in a More-than-Human World* (New York: Vintage Books, 1996), 94.

15. Mary Montaño. *Tradiciones Nuevomexicanas: Hispano Arts and Culture of New Mexico* (Albuquerque: University of New Mexico Press, 1989), 237.

16. Ibid., 239.

17. Ana Castillo, *Massacre of the Dreamers: Essays on Xicanisma*. (New York: Plume Books, 1994), 152.

18. Championed by President Benito Juárez in nineteenth-century Mexico, reforms reappropriated church lands and condemned the usury and elitism of the ecclesiastic hierarchy. The tradition of protesting the church's abuses is seen in the Chicano Movement when the group Católicos por la Raza (Catholics for the Race) opposed the leadership of Cardinal McIntyre and the stratification of church spending in rich and poor neighborhoods. See Mike Davis, *City of Quartz* (London: Verso, 1990), 334–35.

19. Rita Cano Alcalá, Virgins, Martyrs, and Whores: Mexican Cultural Icons of Womanhood in Chicana Literature (Ann Arbor, MI: UMI Dissertation Services, 1999), 242.

20. Paul Vanderwood, *The Power of God against the Guns of Government* (Stanford: Stanford University Press, 1992), 163.

21. Luis Alberto Urrea, *The Hummingbird's Daughter* (New York: Little, Brown, 2006).

22. Gay Wilentz, *Healing Narratives: Women Writers Curing Cultural Dis-ease* (New Brunswick: Rutgers University Press, 2000), 3.

23. Roberto Fernández Retamar, *Caliban and Other Essays* (Minneapolis: University of Minnesota Press, 1989), 19.

24. William Curry Holden, *Teresita* (Owings Mills, MD: Stemmer House, 1978), 148.

Bibliography

Abram, David. *The Spell of the Sensuous: Perception and Language in a More-than-Human World*. New York: Vintage Books, 1997.

Acuña, Rudolfo. *Occupied America: A History of Chicanos*. 3rd ed. New York: Harper and Row, 1988.

Adams, Richard E. W. *Prehistoric Mesoamerica*. Norman: University of Oklahoma Press, 1992.

Alarcón, Norma. "Chicana Feminism: In the Tracks of 'The' Native Woman." In *Living Chicana Theory,* edited by Carla Trujillo. Berkeley, CA: Third Woman Press, 1998.

Alcalá, Rita Cano. *Virgins, Martyrs, and Whores: Mexican Cultural Icons of Womanhood in Chicana Literature*. Ann Arbor, MI: UMI Dissertation Services, 1999.

Anaya, Rudolfo. *Bless Me, Ultima*. Berkeley: TQS, 1972.

Anzaldúa, Gloria. *Borderlands/La frontera: The New Mestiza*. San Francisco: Aunt Lute Books, 1987.

Arenal, Electa, and Amanda Powell, eds. *The Answer/La Respuesta*. By Sor Juana Ines de la Cruz. New York: Feminist Press, 1994.

Arvigo, Rosita, and Nadine Epstein. *Sastun: One Woman's Apprenticeship with a Maya Healer and Their Efforts to Save the Vanishing Tradition of Rainforest Medicine*. San Francisco: Harper, 1995.

Bainton, Roland H. *Hunted Heretic: The Life and Death of Michael Servetus, 1511–1553*. New ed. Providence: Blackstone Editions, [1953] 2005.

Baker, Keith Michael, and Peter Hanns Reill. *What's Left of Enlightenment? A Postmodern Question*. Stanford, CA: Stanford University Press, 2001.

Barnes, Michael Horace. *Stages of Thought*. Oxford: Oxford University Press, 2000.

Boege, Eckart. *Los mazatecos ante la nación*. Mexico City: Siglo veintiuno editores, 1988.

Bonfil Batalla, Guillermo. *Mexico Profundo: Reclaiming a Civilization*. Translated by Phillip A. Dennis. Austin: University of Texas Press, 1996.

Brooke, Elizabeth. *Women Healers: Portraits of Herbalists, Physicians, and Shamans*. Rochester, VT: Healing Arts Press, 1995.

Browner, Carole. "The Management of Reproduction in an Egalitarian Society." In *Women as Healers: Cross-Cultural Perspectives*, edited by Carol McClain, 58–71. London: Rutgers University Press, 1989.

Broyles-González, Yolanda. "Indianizing Catholicism: Chicana/India/Mexicana Indigenous Practices in Our Image." In *Chicana Traditions*, edited by Norma E. Cantú and Olga Nájera-Ramírez. Urbana: University of Illinois Press, 2002.

Buck, Sarah. "The Meaning of the Women's Vote in Mexico, 1917–1953." In *The Women's Revolution in Mexico, 1910–1953,* edited by Stephanie Mitchell and Patience A. Schell. Plymouth, UK: Rowman and Littlefield, 2007.

Buckley, Thomas, and Alma Gottlieb, eds. *Blood Magic: The Anthropology of Menstruation*. Berkeley: University of California Press, 1988.

Bucko, Raymond A. *The Lakota Ritual of the Sweat Lodge: History and Contemporary Practice*. Lincoln: University of Nebraska Press, 1998.

Burkhart, Louise M. "Mexica Women on the Home Front: Housework and Religion in Aztec Mexico." *Indian Women of Early Mexico,* edited by Susan Schroeder, Stephanie Wood, and Robert Haskett. Norman: University of Oklahoma Press, 1997.

Camp, Claudia. *Wise, Strange and Holy: The Strange Woman and the Making of the Bible*. London: Continuum International, 2000.

Campos, Virginia, Armando Sánchez Reyes, Paolo Femia, Alfredo Navarro Magdaleno, Erique Erosa Solana, Daisy Mary Bonilla Contreras, and Marina del Socorro Domínguez Hernández. *La medicina tradicional de los pueblos indígenas de México*. Mexico City: Instituto Nacional Indigenista, 1994.

Canclini, Nestor García. *Hybrid Cultures: Strategies for Entering and Leaving Modernity*. Translated by Christopher L. Chiappari and Silvia L. López. Minneapolis: University of Minnesota Press, 1995.

———. *Transforming Modernity: Popular Culture in Mexico*. Translated by Lidia Lozano. Austin: University of Texas Press, 1993.

Carrasco, David. *Religions of Mesoamerica: Cosmovision and Ceremonial Centers.* San Francisco: Harper Collins, 1990.

Castillo, Ana. *So Far from God*. New York: W. W. Norton, 1993.

Castillo, Debra A. *Talking Back: Toward a Latin American Feminist Literary Criticism*. Ithaca: Cornell University Press, 1992.

Clendinnen, Inga. *Aztecs: An Interpretation*. Cambridge: Cambridge University Press, 1991.

Cosminsky, Sheila. "Maya Midwives of Southern Mexico and Guatemala." In *Mesoamerican Healers,* edited by Brad H. Huber and Alan R. Sandstrom, 179–210. Austin: University of Texas Press, 2001.

Cotera, Marta. "Feminism: The Chicana and Anglo Versions: A Historical Analysis." In *Twice a Minority: Mexican American Women,* edited by Margarita B. Melville, 217–34. St. Louis: Mosby, 1980.

Cruz, Ricardo. "Católicos por la Raza Papers." California Ethnic and Multicultural Archives, University of California at Santa Barbara, Box 15, Folder 6.

Dangler, Jean. *Mediating Fictions: Women Healers and the Go-Between in Medieval and Early Modern Iberia*. Cranbury, NJ: Bucknell University Press, 2001.

Davis, Mike. *City of Quartz*. London: Verso, 1990.

Denevan, William M. *The Native Population in the Americas in 1492*. Madison: University of Wisconsin Press, 1992.

Díaz del Castillo, Bernal. *The Conquest of New Spain*. New York: Penguin Classics, 1963.

Dobyns, Henry F. *Their Number Become Thinned: Native American Population Dynamics in Eastern North America*. Knoxville: University of Tennessee Press, 1983.

Dow, James W. "Central and North Mexican Shamans." In *Mesoamerican Healers*, edited by Brad H. Huber and Alan R. Sandstrom, 66–94. Austin: University of Texas Press, 2001.

Durán, Diego. *Book of the Gods and Rites and the Ancient Calendar*. Translated by Fernando Horcasitas and Doris Heyden. Norman: University of Oklahoma Press, 1971.

——. *The History of the Indies of New Spain*. Translated by Doris Heyden. Norman: University of Oklahoma Press, 1994.

Estrada, Álvaro. *María Sabina: Her Life and Chants*. Translated by Henry Munn. Santa Barbara: Ross-Erikson, 1981.

Fanon, Frantz. *The Wretched of the Earth*. Translated by Constance Farrington. New York: Grove, 1963.

Fardon, Richard. *Counterworks: Managing the Diversity of Knowledge*. London: Routledge, 1995.

Favreau, Pierre, and Salvador Roquet. *Los alucinógenos: De la concepción indígena a una nueva psicoterapia*. Mexico City: Ediciones Prisma, 1981.

Feinberg, Benjamin. *The Devil's Book of Culture*. Austin: University of Texas Press, 2003.

——. "A Toyota in Huautla: Metacultural Discourse in the Sierra Mazateca of Oaxaca, Mexico." Diss. University of Texas at Austin, 1996. Ann Arbor: UMI, 1996. 9705833.

Franco, Jean. *Plotting Women: Gender and Representation in Mexico*. New York: Columbia University Press, 1989.

Furst, Jill Leslie McKeever. *The Natural History of the Soul in Ancient Mexico*. New Haven: Yale University Press, 1995.

Gage, Matilda Joslyn. *Women, Church and State*. Watertown, MA: 1893. Persephone Press, 1980.

Gaspar de Alba, Alicia. "There's No Place like Aztlán: Embodied Aesthetics in Chicana Art." *New Centennial Review* 4, no. 2 (2004): 103–40.

Giddens, Anthony. *Capitalism and Modern Social Theory: An Analysis of the Writings of Marx, Durkheim and Max Weber*. Cambridge: Cambridge University Press, 1971.

Giles, Mary E. *Women in the Inquisition: Spain and the New World*. Baltimore: Johns Hopkins University Press, 1999.

Gómez-Peña, Guillermo. *Dangerous Border Crossers*. New York: Routledge, 2000.

Greenleaf, Richard E. "Historiography of the Mexican Inquisition: Evolution of Interpretations and Methodologies." In *Cultural Encounters: The Impact of the Inquisition in Spain and the New World*. Edited by Mary Elizabeth Perry and Anne J. Cruz. Berkeley: University of California Press, 1991.

Harris, Marvin. *Cannibals and Kings: Origins of Cultures*. New York: Vintage Books, 1977.

Hernández Sáenz, Luz María, and George M. Foster. "Curers and Their Cures in Colonial New Spain and Guatemala: The Spanish Component." In *Mesoamerican Healers*, edited by Brad H. Huber and Alan R. Sandstrom. Austin: University of Texas Press, 2001.

———. *Learning to Heal: The Medical Profession in Colonial Mexico, 1767–1831*. American University Studies. Series 21, Regional Studies, vol. 17. New York: Peter Lang, 1997.

Hill, Jane H. "Women's Speech in Modern Mexicano." In *Language, Gender, and Sex in Comparative Perspective,* edited by Susan U. Philips, Susan Steele, and Christine Tanz, 121–60. Cambridge: Cambridge University Press, 1987.

Holden, William Curry. *Teresita*. Owings Mills, Maryland: Stemmer House, 1978.

Holland, William R. *Medicina maya en los altos de Chiapas*. Translated by Daniel Cazes. Mexico, DF: Instituto Nacional Indigenista, 1963.

Holler, Jacqueline. "More Sins than the Queen of England: Marina de San Miguel before the Mexican Inquisition." In *Women in the Inquisition: Spain and the New World,* edited by Mary E. Giles, 209–29. Baltimore: Johns Hopkins University Press, 1999.

Joyce, Rosemary A. *Gender and Power in Prehispanic Mesoamerica*. Austin: University of Texas Press, 2000.

Karttunen, Frances. "Rethinking Malinche." In *Indian Women of Early Mexico,* edited by Susan Schroeder, Stephanie Wood, and Robert Haskett. Norman: University of Oklahoma Press, 1997.

Kingsley, Peter. *Reality*. Inverness, CA: Golden Sufi Center, 2003.

Kirk, Stephanie L. *Convent Life in Colonial Mexico: A Tale of Two Communities*. Gainesville: University Press of Florida, 2007.

Klein, Cecelia. "Fighting with Femininity: Gender and War in Aztec Mexico." In *Gender Rhetorics: Postures of Dominance and Submission in History,* edited by Richard C. Trexler. Binghamton, NY: Center for Early Medieval and Renaissance Studies, Binghamton State University of New York, 1994.

———, ed. *Gender in Pre-Hispanic Mesoamerica*. Washington, DC: Dumbarton Oaks Research Library Collection, 2001.

Klor de Alva, J. Jorge. "Colonizing Souls: The Failure of the Indian Inquisition and the Rise of Penitential Discipline." In *Cultural Encounters: The Impact of the Inquisition in Spain and the New World,* edited by Mary Elizabeth Perry and Anne J. Cruz. Berkeley: University of California Press, 1991.

Krivitsky, Samuel Karchmer. "La ginecología y la obstétrica." In *Contribuciones mexicanos al conocimiento medico,* edited by Hugo Aréchega and Juan Somolinos Palencia. Mexico City: Fondo de Cultura Económica, 1993.

Lavrin, Asunción, ed. *Latin American Women: Historical Perspectives*. Westport, CT: Greenwood Press, 1978.

Leal, Luis. "Chicano Literary History: Origin and Development." Julian Samora Research Institute Occasional Paper no. 8. East Lansing: Michigan State University, 1996.

Le Dœuff, Michèle. Translated by Trista Selous. *Hipparchia's Choice: An Essay Concerning Women, Philosophy, Etc*. Oxford: Blackwell Press, 1991.

León-Portilla, Miguel. *The Aztec Image of Self and Society: An Introduction to Nahuatl Culture*. Edited by J. Jorge Klor de Alva. Salt Lake City: University of Utah Press, 1992.

———. *Aztec Thought and Culture: A Study of the Ancient Nahuatl Mind*. Translated by Jack Emory Davis. Norman: University of Oklahoma Press, 1963.

Lockhart, James. *The Nahuas after the Conquest: A Social and Cultural History of the Indians of Central Mexico, Sixteenth through Eighteenth Centuries*. Stanford, CA: Stanford University Press, 1992.

López Austin, Alfredo. *Augurios y abusiones*. Mexico, DF: Universidad Nacional Autónoma de México, 1969.

———. "Cuarenta clases de magos del mundo náhuatl." In *Estudios de cultura náhuatl,* vol. 7, pp. 87–117. Mexico, DF: 1968.

———. *Cuerpo humano e ideología: Las concepciones de los antiguos nahuas*. Mexico, DF: Universidad Nacional Autonoma de México, 1989.

———. *The Myths of the Opossum: Pathways of Mesoamerican Mythology*. Translated by Thelma Ortiz de Montellano and Bernard Ortiz de Montellano. Albuquerque: University of New Mexico Press, 1993.

———. *Textos de medicina náhuatl*. Mexico, DF: Universidad Nacional Autonóma de México, 2000.

Macías, Anna. *Against All Odds: The Feminist Movement in Mexico to 1940*. Westport, CT: Greenwood Press, 1982.

McKendrick, Geraldine, and Angus MacKay. "Visionaries and Affective Spirituality during the First Half of the Sixteenth Century." In *Cultural Encounters: The Impact of the Inquisition in Spain and the New World,* edited by Mary Elizabeth Perry and Anne J. Cruz. Berkeley: University of California Press, 1991.

Mignolo, Walter D. *Coloniality, Subaltern Knowledges, and Border Thinking: Local Theories/Global Designs*. Princeton: Princeton University Press, 2000.

Mirandé, Alfredo, and Evangelina Enríquez. *La Chicana: The Mexican-American Woman*. Chicago: University of Chicago Press, 1979.

Molina, Alonso de. *Vocabulario en lengua castellana y mexicana y mexicana y castellana*. Mexico City: Porrua, 1970.

Montaño, Mary. *Tradiciones Nuevomexicanas: Hispano Arts and Culture of New Mexico*. Albuquerque: University of New Mexico Press, 1989.

Moreno de los Arcos, Roberto. "New Spain's Inquisition for Indians from the Sixteenth to the Nineteenth Century." In *Cultural Encounters: The Impact of the Inquisition in Spain and the New World,* edited by Mary Elizabeth Perry and Anne J. Cruz. Berkeley: University of California, 1991.

Muriel, Josefina. *Cultura femenina novohispana*. Mexico City: Universidad Nacional Autónoma de México, 1982.

———. *Los recogimientos de mujeres: Respuesta a una problemática social novohispana*. Mexico: Universidad Nacional Autónoma de México, 1974.

Myers, Kathleen. "Testimony for Canonization or Proof of Blasphemy?" In *Women in the Inquisition: Spain and the New World,* edited by Mary E. Giles, 270–97. Baltimore: Johns Hopkins University Press, 1999.

Niemeyer, E. Victor Jr. *Revolution at Querétaro: The Mexican Constitutional Convention of 1916–1917*. Austin: University of Texas Press, 1974.

Nietzsche, Friedrich. *Beyond Good and Evil*. Translated by Helen Zimmern. Buffalo, NY: Prometheus Books, 1989.

Olcott, Jocelyn. *Revolutionary Women in Postrevolutionary Mexico*. Durham, NC: Duke University Press, 2005.

Ortiz de Montellano, Bernard. *Aztec Medicine, Health, and Nutrition*. New Brunswick: Rutgers University Press, 1990.

Page Pliego, Jaime Tomás. *El mandato de los dioses: Medicina entre los Tzotziles de Chamula y Chenalhó, Chiapas*. Mexico, DF: Universidad Nacional Autónoma de México, 2005.

Paz, Octavio. *Sor Juana Inés de la Cruz o las Trampas de la fe*. Mexico City: Editorial Seix Barral, 1982.

Perry, Mary Elizabeth, and Anne J. Cruz. *Cultural Encounters: The Impact of the Inquisition in Spain and the New World*. Berkeley: University of California Press, 1991.

Platinga, Alvin, and Nicholas Wolterstorff, eds. *Faith and Rationality*. Notre Dame, IN: University of Notre Dame Press, 1983.

Quesada, Noemi. "The Inquisition's Repression of Curanderos." In *Cultural Encounters: The Impact of the Inquisition in Spain and the New World,* edited by Mary Elizabeth Perry and Anne J. Cruz, 37–57. Berkeley: University of California Press, 1991.

Quiñones Keber, Eloise. *Representing Aztec Ritual: Performance, Text, and Image in the Work of Sahagún*. Boulder: University Press of Colorado, 2002.

Retamar, Roberto Fernández. *Caliban and Other Essays*. Minneapolis: University of Minnesota Press, 1989.

Ruíz, Maria. "Border Narratives, HIV/AIDS, and Latina/o Health in the United States: A Cultural Analysis." *Feminist Media Studies* 2, no. 1 (2002): 37–62.

Ruiz, Vicki L. *From out of the Shadows: Mexican Women in Twentieth-Century America*. 10th anniv. ed. New York: Oxford University Press, 2008.

Ruíz de Alarcón, Hernando. *Aztec Sorcerers in Seventeenth Century Mexico: The Treatise on Superstitions by Hernando Ruíz de Alarcón*. Translated and edited by Michael D. Coe and Gordon Whittaker. Albany: State University of New York at Albany, 1982.

Sabat-Rivers, Georgina. "A Feminist Rereading of Sor Juana's *Dream*." In *Feminist Perspectives on Sor Juana Inés de la Cruz,* edited by Stephanie Merrim. Detroit: Wayne State University Press, 1999.

Sahagún, Bernardino de. *Florentine Codex.* Translated by Arthur J. O. Anderson and Charles E. Dibble. Salt Lake City: University of Utah Press, 1953.

Sassen, Saskia. *Globalization and Its Discontents*. New York: New Press, 1998.

Schechner, Richard. *The Future of Ritual: Writings on Culture and Performance*. London: Routledge, 1993.

———. *Performance Theory*. New York: Routledge, 1988.

Scott, James C. *Domination and the Arts of Resistance: Hidden Transcripts*. New Haven: Yale University Press, 1990.

Seler, Eduard. *Collected Works in Mesoamerican Linguistics and Archaeology*. Culver City, CA: Labryinthos, 1991.

Soto, Shirlene. *Emergence of the Modern Mexican Woman: Her Participation in Revolution and the Struggle for Equality*. Denver: Arden Press, 1990.

Taylor, Diana. *The Archive and the Repertoire: Performing Cultural Memory in the Americas*. Durham, NC: Duke University Press, 2003.

Tibón, Gutierre. *Los ritos mágicos y trágicos de la pubertad femenina*. Mexico City: Editorial Diana, 1984.

Tomlinson, John. *Globalization and Culture*. Chicago: University of Chicago Press, 1999.

Torquemada, Juan de. *Monarquía indiana*. Mexico City: Universidad Nacional Autónoma de Mexico, 1971.

Trueblood, Alan S. *A Sor Juana Anthology*. Cambridge: Harvard University Press, 1988.

Tudela, Elisa Sampson Vera. *Colonial Angels: Narratives of Gender and Spirituality in Mexico, 1580–1750*. Austin: University of Texas Press, 2000.

Tuñón Pablos, Julia. *Women in Mexico: A Past Unveiled*. Translated by Alan Hynds. Austin: University of Texas Press, 1999.

Urrea, Luis Alberto. *The Hummingbird's Daughter*. New York: Little, Brown, 2006.

Vanderwood, Paul. *The Power of God against the Guns of Government*. Stanford, CA: Stanford University Press, 1992.

Vélez-Ibáñez, Carlos G. "Carlos G. Vélez-Ibáñez Sterilization Papers ca. 1972–1979." Chicano Studies Research Center Library, University of California at Los Angeles.

Viesca Treviño, Carlos. "*Curanderismo* in Mexico and Guatemala: Its Historical Evolution from the Sixteenth to the Nineteenth Century." In *Mesoamerican Healers,* edited by Brad H. Huber and Alan R. Sandstrom, 47–65. Austin: University of Texas Press, 2001.

———. *Ticiotl: Conceptos médicos de los antiguos mexicanos*. Mexico City: Universidad Nacional Autónoma de México, 1997.

Voss, Stuart. "Nationalizing the Revolution: Culmination and Circumstance." In *Provinces of the Revolution: Essays on Regional Mexican History, 1910–1929,* edited by Thomas Benjamin and Mark Wasserman, 273–317. Albuquerque: University of New Mexico Press, 1990.

Wall, Steve. *Wisdom's Daughters*. New York: Harper Collins, 1993.

Wilentz, Gay. *Healing Narratives: Women Writers Curing Cultural Dis-ease*. New Brunswick: Rutgers University Press, 2000.

Young, James Clay. *Medical Choice in a Mexican Village*. New Brunswick: Rutgers University Press, 1981.

Index

About the Author

Paloma Martinez-Cruz, PhD, is Assistant Professor of Spanish and teaches language, literature, and Latino Studies at North Central College in Naperville, Illinois. She received her BA in Latin American Literature and Chicano Studies from the University of California at Berkeley, and her PhD in Latin American Literature from Columbia University in the City of New York. She published her translation of Conçeicão Evaristo's Brazilian novel *Ponciá Vicencio* with Host Publications in the spring of 2007. With coauthor Liza Ann Acosta, Martinez-Cruz's article "El Macho: A Performance Perspective Which Tells How the Women of Teatro Luna Became Men" will appear in *Performing the U.S. Latino Borderlands,* to be released by Indiana University Press in 2011. Her creative and scholarly writings have been featured in *PALABRA, Nerter* (Canary Islands), *Voces,* and *Ariel Journal.* A Chicago-based writer from North East Los Angeles, she is a resident of the Pilsen community.